The Atlantis Legacy

Taking Humanity Through 2012 and Beyond

Jennifer Hoffman

An imprint of Feed Your Muse Press, LLC

www.feedyourmuse.com

The Atlantis Legacy – Taking Humanity Through 2012 and Beyond

Copyright © 2012 by Jennifer Hoffman.

All rights reserved. All rights reserved. This document is protected by U.S. and international copyright law. No part of this book may be reproduced or transmitted, in whole or in part, in any form or by any means whatsoever, electronic or mechanical, including photocopying, recording or by any information storage or retrieval system, or represented in any form, via print, electronic or other media, without express permission in writing from the publisher, except by a reviewer who may quote brief passages in a published review.

Printed in the USA and distributed by Feed Your Muse Press, LLC. For more information visit us at www.enlighteninglife.com

Feed Your Muse Press, LLC
A Division of Enlightening Life OmniMedia, Inc.
P.O. Box 7076
Lee's Summit, Missouri 64064 USA

Cover design by Katie Sweetman

ISBN 10 0-9821949-4-3

ISBN 13 978-0-9821949-4-2

Dedication

This book is dedicated to those
who have spent lifetimes
preparing themselves and the world
for this moment.
The time has come, the moment is here.
Dream big for yourself and for the world,
for it is through our dreams
that we hear the voice of our heart,
reminding us of who we are,
why we are here,
what is possible, and
what we can achieve
as we ascend into
higher dimensions of being
to create heaven on earth
Together.

Other Titles by Jennifer Hoffman

Books:
30 Days to Everyday Miracles
The Difference Between a Victor and a Victim is I AM
Be Who You Are -- and Fearlessly Live Your True Purpose
The E-Business Primer, a Guide to Business in the Digital Age

CDs:
Cord Cutting and Healing Meditation
Chakra Clearing Meditation
Communicating with your Angels and Spirit Guides
Maternal Emotional Energetic Imprint Clearing

Audio Programs:
Guilt and Shame Healing and Transformation
Aligning the Trinity
The Path of Spiritual Initiation
Manifesting Your Mastery
12 Universal Laws

For additional titles please visit www.enlighteninglife.com

Foreword

Dear Reader,

As I write this we are in the midst of global change and many people are afraid. We have the capability to destroy the world many times over, pollute our water and air, manipulate the weather, create economic chaos, and alter the path of our entire civilization. And while some of these things happen, they do not happen on a scale that disrupts the world to the extent that we experienced in Atlantis. Why not? Is it because deep within our memory we know that there is a fine line that we should not cross?

Do we have a collective memory of our Atlantis Legacy and we avoid going too far in that direction? Despite our belief that we live in a materialistic, ego-centric world that has a marginal interest in its spiritual heritage, is there an undercurrent of spiritual awareness that prevents us from doing irreversible, irreparable harm to ourselves and the planet?

In spite of all of the terrible things we can do with our time, energy and resources, we also have the capability to create good in the world. We can create heaven on earth, become loving stewards of our beautiful planet, ensure that we live in a fair, compassionate, and kind world, provide everyone with the physical, emotional, material, and spiritual sustenance they need to live a fulfilling, rewarding, and abundant life.

Our Atlantis Legacy reminds us of what is possible when we remove spiritual awareness from human action and understanding. It was the end of a process of ascension, an evolutionary journey of healing, learning, growth and transformation in which we could choose the outcome. And we did make a choice, for destruction and annihilation. We are faced with a similar choice in this juncture of our current ascension cycle, a choice whose consequences can be no less dire or disastrous than the one we made in Atlantis. We make this choice every day and as we go through these final moments of this cycle, we are choosing the end as well as the beginning. Will we choose heaven on earth this time, or start another cycle of chaos?

I hope that what you read here helps you make choices in your life, to choose your own heaven on earth and a life filled with abundant blessings. Your Atlantis legacy is a tool for making this choice, and an opportunity to choose higher dimensions of being for yourself, for humanity and for the world.

Many blessings,

Jennifer Hoffman
August 2012

Table of Contents

From Atlantis to Today 1

What is Ascension? 7

The Ascension Cycles 15

Our Ascending Universe 19

Pangea, Lemuria and Atlantis 21

The Atlantean Paradigm 27

Your Atlantis Legacy 31

The Atlantis Feminine Legacy 33

The Atlantis Emotional Legacy 37

The Atlantis Energy Legacy 41

The Destruction of Atlantis 45

The Aftermath and The New Cycle 55

Your Atlantis Lessons 61

The Atlantean Guilt 67

Atlantean Soul Groups 71

The Intention for Ascension 75

Integrating the Healing 77

Healing the Feminine & Masculine 85

Healing Your Atlantean Fear 89

Reclaiming Your Atlantis Gifts 97

Release Soul Group Commitments 105

Clearing the Atlantis Legacy 109

Forgiving Atlantis 115

Clearing your Soul Group Legacy 115

Healing the Energy Connection 117

Connecting with the Full Expression of Your Power 118

Reveal your Power Expression to your Soul Group 119

Release Your Soul Group From Your Shared Legacy 120

Expand Yourself to Match Your Energy 121

Set a New Intention for your Life 122

Forgive and Release All Atlantis Energy 123

The Source Forgiveness Exercise 125

Connecting with the 5th Dimension 127

Ascension -- Our Next Steps 131

Final Thoughts For A New Beginning 138

Question and Answer 141

About the Author 153

From Atlantis to Today

Once upon a time the world's people were preparing for a major event that they knew would change life on the Earth and throughout the universe. It was an exciting time that held many promises for the world and its people, who would live in abundance, joy, peace, and harmony once this transformation was complete. Everyone had done their part to ensure that they were aligned with and prepared for the wonderful transformation that was about to occur. They had even appointed leaders whom they trusted and believed would ensure that this transition would happen in the smoothest and best way possible. Everyone cooperated with the leaders and believed in their integrity and intentions.

And then, something happened as they neared the end of this long journey that had been so anticipated and on which so much depended. The transition went horribly wrong and instead of the beginning of a new world, it was the catastrophic end of the old one. A massive cataclysm destroyed the world and humanity, in an event that reverberated throughout the Universe. The few who survived watched helplessly as millions perished. In a matter of minutes, the once lush and beautiful landscape of the Earth was inundated with water and a new Earth was born, ready for another transformation cycle.

The survivors made a promise, as they watched the horror of the Earth's destruction unfold before them, that they would never allow this to happen again. The next cycle of transformation would be completely different than the previous one so the Earth and its people were not destroyed like this again and they would do everything they could to control the process so it went smoothly. And another ascension cycle began.

If you are wondering what this story is about, it is about the destruction of Atlantis, which ended the most recent Earth ascension cycle. We have experienced several of these ascension cycles and each one has ended with the destruction of an aspect of the Earth and its people. Why would this happen, when so much depended on it? How could such an important transition turn into such a disaster?

With each ascension cycle there is a transition point, a point where ascension and moving into higher dimensions of being must be chosen by each individual. The final outcome doesn't rest on the choice of a single person but each person's choice is important to the overall outcome. In every ascension cycle the point of transition requires that we are willing to move forward by integrating our human presence with our spiritual heritage, integrate our humanity and our divinity, to activate the highest energies within us. And this important point becomes the point of failure if we cannot override the ego's fear of annihilation as we move from an ego-led path into one that is spirit guided. It is a process that is empowered by trust and faith, and not by control. This was the lesson learned in Atlantis and it is the legacy we bring into the current ascension cycle.

In the case of the Atlantis ascension cycle, the energy that would empower ascension was transferred to leaders who were entrusted with the power to control the process. It was their ego-based choices that caused Atlantis' destruction. Instead of working for the collective transition into ascension and ensuring its benefit for all of humanity, they used the power for their own agendas and to further their desire for power and control. But there were other reasons for this failure, including resentment and fear, power imbalances and domination.

Do these sound like familiar topics in light of today's world events? They should because we are replaying the events that took place in Atlantis now; this is our Atlantis Legacy. Time and time again, the highly anticipated promise of ascension for the Earth and its people has always ended in destruction for the same reasons.

We are now at the end of another ascension cycle and very close to the same transition point that became Atlantis' destruction. The fulfillment of ascension, the peace, abundance, joy, love, and harmony that can be possible for all of the Earth and its people is a very likely outcome. And yet the potential for destruction is equally possible. Will we repeat what happened in Atlantis? Can we successfully complete this ascension cycle and move into higher dimensions of being? That depends on many things. I believe that we can and while the potential is there, the final result is yet to be determined.

Much of what you read in this book will be very familiar to you, as you have been part of the Atlantis ascension cycle and probably other ascension cycles before it. In the Atlantean cycle you either lost your life, or were one of the few survivors. You may have worked hard to ensure that the Atlantis ascension cycle was successful or you were one of those responsible for the Earth's destruction. And as you read about Atlantis and the ascension cycle, and realize your Atlantis Legacy, you may experience many emotions and feel anger, sadness, powerlessness, guilt, shame, and fear, or wonder why you are even bothering with this now because you know the outcome will not be successful yet again.

Everything that is happening in the earth today can either remind us of the futility of our efforts against those who seem to want to destroy the planet, or we can be reminded of Atlantis' lessons, that we are each responsible for ascension and there is no one who can individually ensure that the promise is fulfilled or not. It is through the strength of a shared, common intention, our conscious and focused goal for ascension to happen in the best way possible, that we will enable this to happen, no matter what appears to be going on in the world today.

You will read about other ascension paradigms, including Pangea and Lemuria, how they ended, what the result of those cycles taught us and how each ascension cycle builds on the remnants of the previous one.

I'll also talk about the Atlantean Paradigm and the Atlantis Legacy, their role in creating the foundation for today's ascension journey, and how we can use them as tools for transformation so we do not repeat the results of previous ascension cycles.

A concept I hope that you take away from this book is that each of us is on our own ascension journey, which contributes to the Earth's ascension cycle, and a wider universal ascension. As we learn, heal, grow and transform, we raise ourselves to higher dimensions of being, aligning with higher energetic frequencies that empowers the ascension process.

The material and information in this book originated from a seminar I taught in May 2012 about healing the Atlantean Paradigm. It wasn't a class I wanted to teach or a subject I was comfortable discussing. In fact, if the subject had not come up in multiple client sessions, with a variety of different clients, and I had not dreamed about it repeatedly over a two week period, I never would have approached it. While I am comfortable with channeling Archangel Uriel, being highly intuitive, seeing angels and spirits, and connecting with energy, talking about Atlantis was way beyond my comfort zone.

Then something interesting happened when I announced the class. I began to hear from newsletter readers and clients about their Atlantean memories and experiences. Many people wrote to me about the recent dreams they had been having about drowning in Atlantis, seeing the destruction of the earth, and being aware of a deep sense of shame and guilt that they felt when they thought about Atlantis and that ascension cycle. These comments confirmed that teaching this class and addressing this subject was the right thing to do and it was happening at exactly the right time.

During the class many people experienced life changing healing that began with activation of the memories of their Atlantis experiences, then sadness and deep grief over what happened at the end of that cycle, followed by profound transformation as they released those beliefs, thoughts and emotions. As they made the connections between that experience and what is currently happening in their lives today, they were able to let go of their Atlantis Legacy. A new vision and purpose for their lives, began to emerge, they could reconnect to their creativity and find new clarity, energy and empowerment for their life path. Projects and ideas that had been on the back burner for years suddenly came to the forefront, along with the energy, motivation and confidence to help them manifest. They discovered, as you will, how powerfully their Atlantis Legacy had limited their lives and disempowered their dreams.

And many people asked for this book so they could have more information, and a way to work with this energetic paradigm, to heal and release it, so we do not repeat the Atlantean destruction experience. There is so much potential for the success or failure of the current ascension cycle, and the final outcome rests with each of us. We have the potential to destroy the world or to elevate it as we complete this ascension cycle. The most powerful option is for us to complete the cycle and to move into higher dimensions of being.

This is why the information contained in this book is so important. With this ascension cycle we have a chance to transform our humanity into a shared experience of divinity, to transcend the third dimension and become the human family once again, together with our galactic community, with a collective intention for ascension, through healing the Atlantean Paradigm and transforming our Atlantis legacy, to create heaven on earth.

What is Ascension?

Do you know what ascension is? In broad terms, it is an energetic journey during which we raise our vibrations to access higher dimensions of being. While we may enjoy material or physical benefits from ascension, which include more joy, abundance, peace, love, harmony, and better physical health and well being, we are energetic beings, living in an energetic Universe so the overall ascension process overall is about energy and its movement.

While we think about ascension in terms of our unique, individual journey or the ascension of the Earth and humanity, it is also a galactic journey. Ascension involves the whole universe, the parts we can see and those we are not aware of. The entire universe, ours and many others, is ascending at this time too, as the Earth's ascension triggers an ascension process that resonates throughout the omniverse. Can we extend our awareness of the universe to include our membership in a much larger galactic community? Our solar system, a group of planets revolving around our Sun, occupies a tiny corner of our galaxy, the Milky Way. It is part of a universe that we know, which is part of another universe we don't know, and so on. The other planets in our solar system have completed their ascension cycles and the last one to go through this process is the Earth.

Our ascension cycle is part of a much larger, wider reaching ascension cycle that involves all the planets in our solar system and beyond, which has been true for all of the other ascension cycles too. And this is why this particular ascension cycle is so important. The Earth's ascension path is the bridge from the third dimension into higher dimensions for our universe, an energetic pathway into new and higher energetic frequencies. Through ascension we shift our energetic vibrations into new and higher levels. Then we can access dimensions beyond the third, which is the dimension of the 'human' human. To access all higher dimensions, we must become 'spiritual' humans, which requires the completion of ascension. From that point we can see, know and communicate with life on other planets and in other universes. Although they currently appear to be dark, inhospitable, and without life that's because we have not yet achieved the level of vibration that will allow us to be aware of what those planets and their life forms really look like. From our third dimensional perspective that isn't possible.

And moreover, we must complete our ascension journey as an act of our free will so we cannot be aware of these other life forms, obtain their help, or learn from their experiences because we have to make the choice to do this and to complete it successfully without their participation, assistance, or interference. But once we have completed our ascension, and maybe even before, we will learn more about our galactic neighbors. And if that sounds a little bit far off for you, believe me—it is. We have long suspected that we are not alone in the Universe. Are we prepared to know that our suspicions were right?

What does this mean for you? You are part of the Earth's ascension cycle and are on an ascension journey right now. In fact, your entire life has been about ascension, as have all of your previous lifetimes. There is no part of your life that is not contributing to the ascension process in some way. Whatever is happening in your life that you could describe as positive or negative, good or bad, is part of your ascension path. Everything that is currently happening on the earth, good or bad, right or wrong, is part of the Earth's ascension cycle.

And our ascension work is accomplished on four levels, in our individual lives, with all of humanity, with the Earth, and with our universe, and with the many universes beyond it. Everything that we do to raise our individual vibration creates the potential for that new vibration for humanity, which also creates a potential for the Earth to achieve that level of vibration, and so on.

Let's talk about what ascension is not. It is not a religious experience, although some can come to the understanding of love, peace, joy, and our spiritual and divine heritage, that are required for ascension, via religion. It is not an alien-led journey, even though some believe that alien participation or interference is part of this journey too. And it is not optional, meaning we cannot decide that we are not going to participate. Even a choice to not participate is part of an ascension path.

As important as this is, one would think that it would be an easy, smooth transition and we would receive all of the information we need to complete it in the best and most wonderful way possible. But that's not the case. This journey can be one of the most difficult, confusing, and frustrating times of your life. It may challenge you in every way, push you to the brink of sanity and beyond, turn your life upside down to the point where anything else would be a welcome option, remove everything from your life until you are left with nothing, create physical, mental, spiritual and emotional issues that you may not feel strong enough to overcome and yet, you will succeed and move beyond all of it.

You will emerge from this process reborn, with new beliefs, attitudes, and understandings about yourself, the world and the universe.

Your heart will be open and you will know a level of peace and joy that you have never known before.

You will be able to see beyond others' pain, sadness and fear, and look deeply into their hearts to connect with their divinity.

You will see yourself as a powerful creator in your life, a master manifestor.

You will know yourself as a divine human being whose divinity can no longer be eclipsed by your humanity.

You will experience life as an unlimited flow of all of the love, abundance, joy, success, and peace you could ever have imagined for yourself, and all you have to do is allow these things to happen and know yourself through your ascension journey and the potential it contains that lies just beyond its completion.

Now before you get excited about the prospects of this unlimited abundance, joy, love, peace and bliss, since your life probably doesn't have all of those things now, you may be asking when it's going to begin. It has already begun and everything you are now experiencing in your life, especially if it has to do with limitation, lack of abundance, peace, love and joy, enormous life challenges and feeling as though every door in your life is slammed in your face, is proof that you are well into this journey.

To explain, let me share some details of my own ascension journey, or what is better described as the path I was trying to take to avoid my ascension journey, which, as I later discovered, was part of my ascension journey after all.

In October 2003 I had a visitation from Archangel Uriel while I was doing a reading for a friend. My friend had interrupted me as I was talking to say that I was glowing and my voice sounded different. When I asked who was present, I heard "Archangel Uriel and I want you to work with me." Since I had no idea who Archangel Uriel was, I went home and looked on the Internet. And my first response to the request was "No, I don't think so. This isn't right for me. I really don't want to have any part of this and there are other teachers, other people who are much more qualified and certainly have done the preparation work that they need to do for this work. You should ask them."

At the time I was pursuing a career in internet technology, doing work that I enjoyed and was accomplished at. I was a technical project manager, doing software development and implementation. In fact, some of the large websites you may use today were some part of some of the projects I worked on. I wrote the first book on the internet and the e-business course curriculum for the University of Phoenix. To fulfill my career goal of becoming a senior vice president in a technology organization, I became experienced in research and development, quality assurance and testing, and managed development groups in IT departments.

That was a great goal except I could never quite achieve it because I was always getting laid off. From 1998 to 2007 I was laid off six times and two of those layoffs happened in less than 12 months. And that doesn't count all of the times the companies I worked for that were shut down, bought out, merged, or my department was closed. While I really liked the corporate world, the corporate world obviously was not the right place for me and it didn't like me very much. When Archangel Uriel visited me on that day in 2004 I was in between jobs... kind of.

At that time had moved to Phoenix, Arizona for a high paying and very high visibility job with a technology company I really wanted to work for. It was my dream job, running an IT operation within a large technology company. Except a month after I arrived in Phoenix they decided they didn't want to hire me after all. That was one of the lowest points of my life, living in a new town with no friends, I had lost my dream job before I had a chance to start, and I had no other job prospects. So there I was, unable to find another job, running out of money, experiencing my first Phoenix summer, and feeling very hopeless and helpless. After many months of searching, the only job I could find was reading tarot cards in a metaphysical bookstore and I don't know anything about reading tarot cards.

I would go to work every day, sure that I was going to tell someone something that was totally wrong, then they would know I was a fraud and had no idea what I was doing, and then I would lose my job, be unable to pay my bills, then I would be homeless, out on the street and totally power-less. At the time I was nearly homeless, was sharing a tiny apartment with my son, sleeping on a twin mattress on the floor. And every night I would tell God that this was not the life I wanted at all, and asked to be taken home. Then I'd wake up in the morning and think 'Darn it, I'm still here.' I did this every night and day for six months.

Then something I never expected happened. Despite my inability to read tarot cards I learned that I am a gifted and very accurate intuitive and within a short time I was the busiest advisor at the store, with a long list of regular customers who came to see me in a steady stream every day. Although I have been intuitive since I was a young child, I had never considered doing that as a job or life path.

And that is where I was in my life on the day that Archangel Uriel came to visit me.

Now I still wanted to do internet technology work, which is why I initially declined to take advantage of Uriel's offer. But if you know anything about the spiritual world, it is relentless, so the requests from Uriel continued on a daily basis until three months later, I said I would work with him on a limited basis.

I would write one newsletter and build a small website.

I would tell a few people about my work with Archangel Uriel.

I would teach a few classes and then I would turn the work over to someone else, who really wanted to do it, while I pursued my technology career.

I've been writing the newsletter for nine years now and it has over two million weekly readers. The website has been up since March of 2004 and gets millions of visitors every month. And I now also host a popular weekly radio show, have taught hundreds of classes, written thousands of articles, shared countless messages and still work with Uriel, nearly ten years later.

This was all part of my ascension journey and through it I was propelled into this work, which is not what I had chosen as my life path. Many of you share similar experiences, where the low point of your life has been the beginning of the journey into healing, learning, growth and transformation that is your ascension path.

And now here we are at yet another ascension crossroads. This is also the completion of a 25,000 year earth cycle and a 250,000 year plus galactic cycle so we are truly at the crossroads of some profound potential for transformation. Which way will we go, upwards into higher dimensions of being or down into the abyss of another cycle of planetary destruction, to be rebuilt for yet another ascension cycle? The entire universe is poised to see what we are going to do as we make our choices about ascension.

If you are looking at all of the doors in your life that have closed, wondering "What do I do now?" take heart, for this is a powerful moment in your life. What you will learn about Atlantis and your role in its ascension cycle will help to make some of those choices but it will also show you how you got to where you are now, the Atlantis legacy that has been limiting you and why the limitations exist. You will also learn what ascension means to you in the scope of your lifetime and the soul group you've chosen and what the promise of ascension really is. Just so you know, it doesn't mean that spaceships will come down from the sky to take the lucky ones away and "Too bad!" for everyone else.

We're focusing on Atlantis in particular because it was the most recent ascension cycle whose results created the foundation for the cycle we are now completing. Each of us who feels an Atlantean connection has consciously or unconsciously participated in the destruction of Atlantis in one way or another. Our role in Atlantis and which side we were on during its destruction determines the inherited legacy, which I refer to as the Atlantis Legacy, which includes the memories and beliefs that we inherited from this lifetime. And the Earth embodies an energetic paradigm, which I call the Atlantean Paradigm that we created for this ascension cycle. The closer we come to the potential for a similar kind of destructive outcome that we experienced in Atlantis, the more our legacy and this paradigm become the focus of our awareness.

Knowing this gives us the insights and tools to change the outcome so we achieve the ending we desire. The soul mates and soul groups, our lifetime partners and teachers, we choose are also part of our Atlantean Legacy. With them we have an opportunity to complete powerful healing with our former Atlantean partners, and this paradigm determines our relationships, energy exchange, interactions, and how we allow ourselves to use our energies and gifts today. Are you reluctant to use your gifts, to experience yourself in higher energies? You can blame this on your Atlantean Paradigm and you will learn how to change it.

The foundation of our ascension cycle today encapsulates the Atlantean Paradigm and our Atlantis Legacy so we will learn about them in detail. Then we will do the healing and transformation work necessary to heal these memories and energetic imprints so we can use our Atlantean connection in a powerful way to bring the promise and blessings of ascension to ourselves, to the family of humanity, to the earth, the galaxy and to the Universe.

The Ascension Cycles

An ascension cycle is a process of spiritual evolution that encompasses cycles of disconnection and reconnection, of rejection and acceptance, of being disconnected and disempowered to reconnection and empowerment. But it's much more than that. It's a cycle of energetic evolution through different dimensions of being along the energetic evolutionary spiral. From our human perspective we consider the physical evolution of the species and see how we have transformed across the ages in response to our changing environment. But we don't consider the energetic implications of this evolution, as there is a corresponding energetic shift in every stage of physical evolution, which is ascension.

These energetic shifts happen across different dimensions of being. While we are aware of three physical dimensions, there are many other dimensions that we cannot imagine or envision. In fact, modern quantum physics now recognizes at least sixteen dimensions. So our awareness of multiple dimensions and the potential for being in different dimensions, beyond the third, currently exists even though we can't see or aren't aware of them to the point where we can establish a meaningful interaction with them. Although, they are able to interact with us in ways we aren't aware of and that is another aspect of both our Atlantean history and our current journey.

Getting to the third dimension was also an ascension journey. While we do not always consider dimensions before the third, they are important when we look at ascension as part of our path of spiritual evolution.

In the first dimension, which is where the Earth started out many, many millennia ago, there was all darkness and no light. Life was not yet a possibility; and there was only matter in its most basic form. The introduction of light raised the first dimension to the second, so darkness had a counterpoint in the light. But there was no structure or form, only chaos.

There was action and reaction, destruction and creation but there was still no life as there was no way to apply energy to create form. The light brought in energy that simply allowed the darkness to expand itself to overcome the light and then allow the light to destroy it.

The second dimension ascended to the third when we add the concept of free will and the ability to move energy by using thought to create form. Now life was possible and with it, the ability to control and direct the flow of energy. The third dimension contained the aspects of the two previous dimensions, light, dark, chaos, and energy, as well as structure and form. This is the dimension of destiny, where energy flows in a pre-determined way and form follows a specific structure which we also call karma or destiny. This is the dimension of humanity and the ego, in which our purpose is linked to our destiny. Our previous destiny leaves an energetic imprint in the Earth's grid which we return to resolve in each lifetime. Our lifetimes are energetic cycles, continuous energetic loops which follow a specific karmic path, until we ascend through the experience and raise it to a different vibration, which releases the karma.

In the third dimension we can apply intentional thought to energy, creating what we know as our reality. And this is where we are today. This can be and often is a highly chaotic process except we have a gift in the third dimension, the ascension path into the fourth and higher dimensions, which is achieved via integrating spirit into the human ego, which is also the purpose of the current ascension cycle.

As we integrate ego and spirit, we align our frequency with the vibration of unconditional love, the highest energetic vibration in the universe. It is through this integration that we bring in the fourth dimension and gain access to dimensions beyond it. Unconditional love, which is an energy and not an emotion, can be used, along with our intention, to deliberately create form and structure, to override fate, destiny, and karma. This opens us to the potential for creation and manifestation far beyond the form and structure of our third dimensional lifetime energy cycles and this is the meaning of heaven on earth.

When we complete this ascension cycle we will fully understand the fourth dimension and those beyond it, which is more than just using intention to create our reality beyond karma. It's understanding ourselves as divine and knowing that we are mirrors of spirit and of the universe. We will embrace the concept of oneness and understand our shared connections within the family of humanity. Then we can take this a step farther to see ourselves as universal, where the universe—the entire universe—is actually embodied within each of us and within everyone else too. This is already mirrored in our physical body, as we have atoms with a nucleus and protons, neutrons, and electrons that orbit around it, which is similar to how the planets in our solar system orbit around our central Sun. We are a microcosm of the macrocosm, a 'wheel within the wheel' as was written in the Bible.

If you know the concept of fractal geometry or fractal mathematics, everything on the earth is a fractal, and each thing is a mirror of every other thing. If you observe a grain of sand under a strong microscope, it resembles the pebbles, rocks, boulders and mountains it came from. Blood runs through our body's veins in the same way that sap runs through a tree's trunk. Each tree leaf resembles the tree structure, with the trunk and branches. That's the concept of connectedness and of oneness, and of oneness in unity with all things. Understanding that requires thinking beyond the third dimension to fully embrace ourselves as a cog in the wheel of the universe. In the third dimension, we think we are the 'king of the world and everything around us' and we feel alone, isolated and separate. But beyond the third dimension, this type of thinking does not exist.

The ascension cycle for the Earth involves all of its inhabitants, including plants, animals and humanity. Rather than travelers, guests, or casual inhabitants of the earth, we are part of the Earth's body and energetic field.

As we begin to consider that the Earth is a sentient being, we become aware of ourselves and all of its inhabitants as part of its physical and energetic body and embrace the connections which create the synergy between us all. In astrology we recognize the energies of the other planets in our solar system as they move through different cycles. Can we extend this to include the Earth and recognize the synergistic impact and influence that we share with it? This further activates the common energetic theme of ascension, which is part of all of our ascension journeys and establishes the commonality of our experiences, purpose, and journey from one state of being and dimension to another.

Now we have to move beyond the Earth and consider our broader connections that resonate through the universes. Can we accept that we are not, and have never been alone, either on our planet or in the Universe? Is it possible for us to see ourselves as galactic and universal citizens? This is also a carryover from Atlantis, which had a strong connection with the galactic community. As we learn more about Atlantis and its ascension cycle we will also see how much our current world reality reflects the legacy of this earlier ascension cycle in ways we have yet to consider. Atlantis has much to teach us about ascension and as we learn about it, we also heal that paradigm, release its legacy, and step closer to initiating the wave of transformation that carries us all towards higher dimensions of being.

Our Ascending Universe

We live in a dynamic universe that's always growing, expanding and ascending. That is hard for us to understand because we live in a finite world with boundaries, limits, endings and stopping points. There is always an 'end of the road' for us, where we have to make a conscious choice to move into another direction. We want to know where the boundary is, when do we get to the 'end', when is it finished or over, or when the energy stops flowing. When does the Universe stop expanding? Is there a universal bucket or sea or pond? How big is it? How big does it get before it overflows its boundaries? What happens then?

The concept of 'limitlessness' isn't easy to understand, especially within a limited dimensional space, like the third dimension. Having a fixed and limited thought process that only allows us to know what we can perceive with our physical senses doesn't help the situation. But whether we can see it or not, the universe is a boundless presence that cannot be defined by time, distance, or matter. While scientists try to look for the ends of the universe, it is constantly expanding, growing ever larger in every direction. There are countless layers of the universe that vary in size, dimension, energy, vibration, light, form, and space. And as the Universe grows in size it expands upwards and downwards, outwards and inwards upon itself. As we complete our ascension cycle other aspects of the universe enter the space we just vacated so they can experience the ascension cycle we just finished. It's a constantly renewing cycle that is endless, limitless, infinite, and everlasting.

As we acknowledge that we are part of a much larger universal ascension cycle we have to avoid losing focus on our own ascension, the one that is part of our life path because it is part of the larger universal ascension path. The completion of our ascension path enables ascension for all. It is what is happening within us now, in the many ways that we're transforming, integrating our learning, empowering ourselves to move into higher dimensions of being, that contributes to the larger ascension cycles of humanity, the Earth, the solar system, the galaxy, and the universe and universes.

What did we learn from previous ascension cycles and how are they integrated into our current path? To know this we need to talk about Pangea, Lemuria and Atlantis.

Pangea, Lemuria and Atlantis

We have had three previous ascension cycles that are important to us today. Each of them achieved a specific level of ascension that was necessary for the next ascension cycle. Although we believe that each ascension cycle has the potential to propel us into higher dimensions, this is an evolutionary process and a quantum shift that happens in a specific order. Once we have achieved ascension beyond the third dimension it is possible for us to ascend into higher dimensions at will. But the path out of the third dimension is the most challenging because it involves the greatest levels of transformation. Each ascension cycle prior to the current one accomplished its own goals and went as far as it could go based on the energy of the earth and its inhabitants at the time. Then the next cycle was built on the foundation set by the previous one.

With the end of the Pangean Cycle the moon split off from the Earth and went shooting off into the sky above it. Have you noticed how the moon controls the earth's water (and we're 95% water), the tides and also rules the emotions? The separation of the Earth and the Moon was the splitting of the emotional self from the physical self, the heart from the mind, which represented the separation of the logical mind and heart. We were no longer able to use our heart/mind connection to make our choices, as rationality became more important than emotions. So we became two separate aspects—one was logical and led by the ego, the other was emotional and led by the heart. We read about this in the Bible's story of Adam and Eve, when they ate from the true of the knowledge of good and evil. The story is they separated from God but the truth is that they separated themselves from the energy of unconditional love.

The second ascension cycle was the Lemurian cycle and it ended with a great cataclysm that split the existing single land mass into seven continents. These continents drifted away from each other to occupy different places on the planet. If you look at a map of the world you can see evidence of where the continents were once joined together, like the pieces of a gigantic jigsaw puzzle.

This was the separation of the family of humanity from itself, and separated our humanity from our divinity. Now there were different cultures, tribes, groups, and societies that forgot their shared connection. Separated by land and water, we were no longer united as a community, and our geographic separation quickly grew into a new paradigm of judgment and discrimination. New energies, such as fear, hate, jealousy, domination, and control, were introduced. From the Lemurian ascension cycle we have the different races, colors, societies, genders, and cultures that we know today. And we live on different continents, speak different languages, have different ways of thinking, we have religious beliefs that separate us from each other and from God, and we see ourselves in terms of gender, color, race and culture rather than the family of humanity. In the Bible, this is reflected in the story of the Tower of Babel. The Lemurian ascension cycle became the foundation for the Atlantis cycle and reconnection was one of its lessons.

Next we had the Atlantean cycle, which is the one we are the most familiar with today. The story of how Atlantis was destroyed is detailed in a later chapter of this book. The purpose of the Atlantean ascension was the reconnection of the family of humanity with each other, the galaxy, the universes and with Source. And to reunite the heart and mind, to bring the emotional body back into alignment and integrated within the physical body and to bring us back into alignment with our wholeness of human and divine. This full integration would have allowed the Earth and humanity full access to the highest energies of unconditional love and raise the frequency of the Earth beyond the fifth dimension and into higher dimensions of being.

Another aspect of Atlantis' ascension was to reunite the masculine and feminine energies in their highest, divine forms. And to reunite humanity with its divine Source, to become the 'spiritual human'.

But it was not to be. There was interference in the form of an ego-led plan to control ascension that once again led to a cataclysm that destroyed the Earth and humanity. Atlantis' destruction also erased millennia of spiritual progress, enlightenment, technology, and social advancement. Its legacy created the Atlantean Paradigm, the energetic memory that includes the beliefs, fears, attitudes, and energies that were created with the destruction of Atlantis. And our integration of this paradigm into our cellular memory, emotional DNA and karmic cycles is our individual and shared Atlantis Legacy.

Beyond the physical destruction, loss of life and damage to the Earth, Atlantis' destruction was doubly traumatic because we really believed that this would be the final ascension cycle. And we were aware enough of the potential for access to higher dimensions to know that it was possible. The dramatic endings of the Pangean and Lemurian cycles were within the potential of their energetic frequencies and they were important aspects of the path that Atlantis had the potential to fulfill.

But before we consider Atlantis a failure, because it was not, we have to consider all of the aspects of healing, learning, growth and transformation that Atlantis was faced with, which were substantial. Even in Atlantis, with all of its wonderful technology, gifts, and abilities, we ascended to the point of our energetic and vibrational potential and not beyond it. But an ascension cycle is not the end of everything, they are renewable. Once we complete the current ascension cycle, there will be another that follows.

Atlantis held a lot more hope for the fulfillment of ascension as the higher vibrations already existed and moving into higher dimensions was seen as highly probably and rather easy. And the Atlantean cycle presented an ascension opportunity for populations from many different planets, dimensions and many different kinds of energetic beings. There was no doubt or question that it was going to happen, which is why its destruction was so much more difficult on many levels. Although that didn't happen in Atlantis, we have a new opportunity with the current ascension cycle.

Today's ascension cycle also includes multitudes of the universes' populations. Have you ever wondered why there are so many people on the planet today? The world's enormous population, around seven billion people, is not the result of overpopulation. It is not because there are too many people having too many children. Have you noticed, when looking at a crowd of people, how many people look like? It's because they are from the same places and that is not limited to places within our Earth's geography.

There are many different intergalactic cultures, races, tribes, energies, and communities present on the Earth today who are from places that are beyond our solar system, galaxy, and universe. They are here because the end of an ascension cycle is occurring and as the final planet to ascend in our solar system and our universe, this is where it's all happening. Everyone who has not previously completed an ascension cycle, who needs the lessons of ascension, who needs to participate in the completion of an ascension cycle, and who needs to do their own ascension work, is present on the Earth now.

While they are present in physical form, their physical body is nothing more than a place holder in the third dimension so they can be here energetically and do the work that only the third dimension can provide, which includes lessons in fear, forgiveness, compassion, and unconditional love. The type of healing, learning, growth and transformation that shifts us from human to divine, that has access to free will so we can choose our divinity and experience unconditional love, is only available in the third dimension.

Many of you have experienced all three cycles, Pangaea, Lemuria, and Atlantis. And it is why you are here today too, as you bring their energetic imprints and memories as reminders of these cycles and to help avoid repeating what we have already experienced. As a member of the Pangean and Lemurian cycles your role may have been to be an enlightened teacher and a source of inspiration in the hope that you could influence humanity to create a different outcome for their ascension path. But you were probably ignored or persecuted for your efforts. You may have tried to influence humanity to shift into a higher dimension than they were capable of achieving at that time and it was a potential choice for them, if they could connect with it. This may also have been your role in Atlantis and it is your role today.

Some of the Earth's extra-galactic inhabitants today have been part of Pangea and Lemuria too, and they bring those energies to this ascension cycle. Whether they are participating in a positive, fulfilling and expansive way or they are playing a negative, blocking, limiting role is part of their purpose here. The ascension process was never intended to be an orderly, pre-planned and orchestrated process. Successful ascension and movement into higher dimensions is not guaranteed. There is no referee to ensure that everything is in place, everything is working, is moving in a forward direction and all systems are 'go'. There is no tour guide to tell us that it is going to be an effortless process and all we have to do is sit back, relax and enjoy the trip because someone is going to take care of the details.

That is something that we would like to have happen but it is not the purpose, intention or path of ascension. It is definitely not the intention for ascension because it is through our ascension journey that we shift energetic paradigms within ourselves and in the universe. There is a lot of healing to be done, from previous ascension cycles and from the karma we have created over lifetimes of separation, fear, domination and control that will happen during this ascension cycle.

Since ascension is an energetic process, its progress depends on how well we manage our energetic frequency and vibration. While the Earth has its own vibration, it also reflects ours and responds to the levels that we are able to generate and maintain. As we become more proficient in managing our vibrational frequency, through our own healing, learning, growth and transformation, we provide the Earth with support on its ascension journey. The Earth reflects back to us the energy we hold and we participate with the Earth in this ascension cycle. The two cannot be separated and must happen simultaneously. We cannot raise our vibration higher than the Earth will allow and the Earth's vibration cannot be higher than that of the collective of humanity. Bear this in mind because it is the reason behind the destruction of Atlantis.

Everyone who played a role in the destruction of Atlantis is also participating in the current ascension cycle. Whether they were the causative factors of the destruction—and we're going to talk about what happened in Atlantis and the details of that particular ascension cycle—or their power was used inappropriately, or they were the innocent bystanders who were part of the collateral damage, they are here now because they get to go through it again. Your Atlantean legacy, your role in the Atlantean cycle, the Atlantean Paradigm that was imprinted in the Earth's energetic field in preparation for this ascension cycle, and what happened to you in those final days and hours, is one of the reasons you chose to be here today, and also chose your soul group, gifts, life path, and karma. Who you were then, what you think you did, what you think you have to atone for, and how you atone for that are all part of the Atlantis Legacy you elected to heal in this lifetime, for yourself, for humanity, the Earth and the universe and to do that you chose the life path that would provide the greatest healing, learning, growth and transformation for our shared ascension journey.

The Atlantean Paradigm

Today's ascension cycle is a chance to try again, as all ascension cycles are, as well as an opportunity to heal the Atlantis legacy and take this cycle in a new direction, for us, our universe, and our galactic community. Failure is not an option, something I don't say lightly or to pressure anyone, but we know we have to succeed. We know that now is the time and this is our moment. We are in this place for a reason and we've learned enough from our previous ascension cycle experiences to be able to do it this time.

How we understand and use our energy today is important in this cycle because we came into our current lifetime with a great deal of energy and power even though we do not use all of it, or even most of it. You have heard scientists talk about how we use about five percent of our brain and the rest does not get used. We will have full use of our brain capacity as we approach the end of this ascension cycle. Scientists recognize two active strands of human DNA but know that we have other, unused strands which they call 'junk DNA'. Humans have a total of twelve strands of DNA, and our twelve strands of DNA will be activated as we complete this ascension cycle.

The higher perspective needed to activate all of our brain functioning and our twelve strands of DNA is achieved as an aspect of our transition into higher dimensions. We see evidence of this movement now, as we are more accepting of spiritual concepts, we are comfortable with the idea of angels and spirits and even see them at times. We are aware that the veil which once acted as a nearly impenetrable wall between the spiritual and material worlds is now nearly non-existent. And we are aware of ourselves as energy in motion, are able to manifest, and to acknowledge the spiritual aspects of ourselves that exist within our humanity. These concepts, once forbidden, are now part of everyday life and conversation.

How we are using our energy to empower or disempower our ascension journey is an integral part of healing our Atlantis Legacy, or Atlantean Paradigm. This is an energetic imprint or template that governs what we must do, or overcome, in this ascension cycle. It is a set of parameters, created at the end of the Atlantis ascension cycle, to govern or manage our use of and access to energy in the next cycle.

Each ascension cycle creates the foundation for the one that follows it. There are certain guidelines or rules that are put in place at the end of an ascension cycle to ensure that its lessons are integrated within the energy of the next one. These rules were created at the end of the Atlantis cycle, so we could fulfill what we had planned to do in that cycle and complete the mission of the next cycle. Each cycle, then, has a dual purpose and this is true of our current cycle. We are here to heal the Atlantean Paradigm, release our Atlantis Legacy, and to ascend into our divinity at the same time. Now do you understand why aspects of this cycle have been so challenging and why it feels as though you are repeating the past while trying to walk forward into the future? If there was ever a time to learn multi-tasking this is definitely it.

Although we had to learn the lessons of Atlantis so we would not repeat them in the current ascension cycle, we knew that we would repeat them. We also knew that we would probably, at some point, do something worse in our current cycle, than we did in Atlantis, because the possibility of going backwards is always present. Sometimes we must revisit the past to remind ourselves of what we want to do in the present. This is both the gift and the curse of the third dimension, the free will which allows us to do anything we wish to do and take our path in any direction we choose. We can choose to be led by our mind, heart, ego, desire for revenge, hurt, pain, joy, love -- it doesn't matter, whatever we choose is where our energy will go. And yet, despite the limitations of our Atlantean Paradigm that we live with, there is a still, small voice which reminds us of the promise of a higher aspect, a different choice that is a chance for a completely new kind of reality for us, the Earth and the universe.

Within the context of our Atlantean Paradigm we limit the use of our gifts and power through fear, guilt, and shame because of our role in Atlantis, or what happened to us there, or both. Our fear of using our full power is part of our Atlantean Paradigm. Although we had a wide range of abilities and gifts we remember how we may have misused this power. Can we trust ourselves with that kind of power and not use it to destroy the Earth and humanity?

Part of how we do and do not use our energy today is limited by our memory of what we did with our gifts and abilities and what was done to us and to Atlantis because of them. There is a lot of guilt and shame involved in the Atlantis Legacy and that's probably one of its most destructive aspects for us. We feel a tremendous amount of guilt over what happened although most of us were not directly responsible for Atlantis' destruction. We are ashamed of our misguided trust and how we allowed our power to be misused. And, depending on our role in the cataclysm, anger over having been so taken advantage of by people we loved and trusted. There is also a considerable amount of shame over having ended the ascension cycle for everyone, including the Earth's population and the galactic community that Atlantis was so closely connected to.

Atlanteans were very aware of their galactic community connections and knew how important their ascension was to the universe. The galactic community watched Atlantis' progress carefully and tried to help as the situation quickly got out of control, much more quickly than they thought could occur. They disaster was of such huge proportions that they were powerless to help and this also created a significant amount of guilt and shame in the universal community as they watched humanity perish by their own hand. Instead of ascension, the planet and civilization were destroyed, as was the hope of ascension for the universe in the Atlantean cycle.

Despite our mission to complete the current ascension cycle and ascend into higher dimensions, creating heaven on earth for ourselves, humanity, and the earth, we entered this ascension cycle with strong limitations on our energy. This is why we have limited access to our brain functioning and only two active DNA strands. There are two reasons for this: first, we had to be part of the Earth in the energetic state we were at when we began the Atlantean experience, not when we ended it. We had to learn all of the lessons of Atlantis again, especially with respect to the use of power and energy. At the point of the final outcome, which is where we are now, we had to experience the full spectrum of learning, growth, healing and transformation that would bring us to the point where we could be faced with some of the same choices we had to make during the end of the Atlantis ascension cycle, and have the energetic potential to make other choices.

Second, we didn't trust ourselves enough to incarnate in this lifetime and at the beginning of this particular ascension cycle with the full use of our power and our abilities. We were too traumatized by what we did with our power, or allowed others to do with it and how it destroyed the planet. Because we didn't trust ourselves to not take that same path and not destroy the Earth before we were fully ready to step into these final stages of the Atlantean Paradigm, we made sure that we did not have the ability to do so. And this is why the more gifted, connected, powerful, intuitive and light-filled we are, the more difficult our journey appears to have been. In some ways, we are making ourselves pay for how our power was misused, even though it was not entirely our fault, by limiting ourselves in every way because we do not trust ourselves and we do not trust others. This is reflected in how we individually integrate the Atlantean Paradigm as our Atlantis Legacy.

Your Atlantis Legacy

The most gifted among us are often those who are the most reluctant to acknowledge their gifts and power and shine their light. Many of you who are light bearers and light workers today were a very important part of Atlantis and its ascension cycle. You shared your light very willingly with people who had their own agenda and who used it for their own purposes. Your light and power were misused, abused and usurped. Rather than using your light to complete the Atlantis cycle, it was used to destroy Atlantis and nearly all of the people in it. Is feeling taken advantage of something you struggle with today? Are you afraid to use your power because you don't want anyone to know how powerful you really are? Do you fear technology and limit its role in your life? It's part of your Atlantean Legacy, the energetic legacy of fear, guilt and shame from your Atlantis lifetime.

Now that you are in a new ascension cycle your Atlantis memories remind you that it is better to not share your light or risk being taken advantage of, so you hide your light where no one can see it. This has been experienced throughout our lifetimes since Atlantis as persecution but it has its basis in our Atlantis Legacy. You will understand this concept more fully when you read about how your light was used to destroy Atlantis.

Although you probably have no reason to feel guilt and shame over your Atlantean past, you do anyway because as light bearers, keepers and teachers of the light you felt responsible for the completion of the ascension cycle. While you innocently and willingly surrendered your light and power for what you thought was a higher purpose, you realized your mistake when it was too late to save everyone, including yourself. Instead of being a powerful force for ascension and for good, those who had worked so hard for ascension helped create Atlantis' destruction.

And you may have mixed feelings about technology and the digital age, including the use of computers and other technical processes. Some of you are afraid of it, others avoid it as much as possible, and others learn only as much as they absolutely have to, in order to function in today's digital world. If this describes you and you think that there must be something wrong with you because you wonder why it seems to easy for everyone else and it is very hard for you, look no farther than your Atlantis Legacy. Technology destroyed Atlantis and this is something you remember so you limit your use of technology and try to stay away from it, even if it limits your life or business. The fear of technology is a strong aspect of the Atlantean Legacy you integrated into your life path.

Through our Atlantis Legacy we humble ourselves, using the most extreme meaning of this word, denying our divine birthright, placing ourselves far beneath the blessings of our divinity and feeling unworthy of a direct Source connection. Our Atlantean Paradigm blueprint included the introduction of religion through which we would separate ourselves from Source and then have to re-learn how to express our divinity in partnership with our humanity. Our humility would extend to how we used our gifts and talents and experienced abundance. We would allow ourselves to be led by others, unaware of our ability to control our own life path, until we found the road to freedom and liberation. All of those aspects that were so abundantly available in Atlantis, would be denied to us until we could reconnect with the light within, in a balanced way. The light was there for us to find, when we were ready to seek it out with open hearts.

The most powerful aspect of the Atlantis legacy is the integration of the masculine and feminine energies. It is why the masculine energy is dominant today because it is the most important aspect we had to heal and transcend in this ascension cycle. The dominance of the female energetic vibration, the nurturing, supportive, loving energy of the feminine, was partly responsible for Atlantis' destruction.

The Atlantis Feminine Legacy

One of the lessons of the Atlantis cycle was to integrate the divine masculine and feminine energies into the male and female aspects of humanity. But this was distorted through the creation of a dominant female presence and a suppressed, less important male presence. The return to the vibration of unconditional love, necessary for ascension into higher dimensions and the integration of this frequency into humanity's energetic field was the mission of the Atlantis ascension cycle. So the feminine energy dominated, thinking that the focus of the nurturing, loving and supportive energy of the feminine would bring the Lemurian legacy into balance. But this was an unbalanced paradigm as well and when the masculine energy of control and domination was put into play, in the form of the ego's use of energy towards the end of the Atlantis cycle, Atlantis was destroyed.

Masculine and feminine energy, when focused through the human, ego-led aspects becomes male and female and is much different from the higher frequencies of these energies, when guided by spirit. In Atlantis the feminine energy was also driven by the ego, which meant this energy was used in a logical, rational and judgmental way. The feminine became the female and was seen as better and more competent than the male. The masculine became male and was viewed as inferior to women. Over time, this created polarity and resentment. While the male energy is effective at creating action and moving energy, without the balancing guidance of spirit, it is expressed through the ego as domination and control.

In the same way, the feminine energy, without the balancing guidance of spirit and expressed through the ego, can be loving but overindulgent, its strength expressed as manipulation, and its support leans towards co-dependence. Women, in Atlantis' days, saw themselves as superior to men, made them subservient, and did not give them a place of importance, honor, and respect in society. Men thought that women were not managing ascension well or effectively and resorted to their own measures to complete ascension. Instead of creating a balance of masculine and feminine energies, they created discord between the male and female aspects, rejected spirit and the result destroyed everyone. But with the discord and imbalance that were created by the division between these two energies, the only solution was to begin again with a new cycle that would learn the lessons of the previous one, to try once again to balance the male and female with spirit. In its highest aspects, the balanced masculine and feminine aspects move and sustain energy in an effortless flow, for the highest good of all.

This is why we have lived through millennia of male control throughout our current ascension cycle. The masculine energy has been allowed to dominate the female the point of total repression so that we could bring these energies back into balance by coming to the point where we were willing to integrate spirit. In the process, the male energy was given a place of prominence and made the dominant energy. The hope was that the male energy would see the need for balance and learn to integrate spirit and merge with its divine feminine. As we know, that did not happen. We have lived through centuries of the total control and domination by the male energy which has created war, suppression, repression, destruction and fear.

In many ways, the male energy has created the same imbalance of power that the female energy did in Atlantis, with similar results. This aspect of our ascension cycle that will play out and it is coming to an end now as the feminine energy begins to rise to the challenge, not against the male energy but in support of a new way of being.

The rise of the feminine energy, which we are now experiencing, is happening as we realize the need for the equal balance of these two energies, where one does not dominate the other. Neither one is more important and both are required to achieve ascension into higher frequencies. Male and female energies, formerly expressed through the ego, must become a balanced expression masculine and feminine energies guided by spirit. We will not ascend as masculine or feminine but as a balanced being with full appreciation, integration, respect and honor for both energies.

Hearing about these Atlantean experiences can be very painfully emotional as you begin to reconnect with who you were and what happened then. This can bring up thoughts of "I should have known better. I had a greater responsibility to use my light in the right way and instead I trusted people that I shouldn't have trusted," and feelings of responsibility. Please bear in mind that you are recalling this information so that it can be put to use at this time, understanding what happened in the past to set more powerful, intentional choices today.

These choices are also part of the ascension process because ascension is both a promise and a purpose.

The promise is of a new opportunity to ascend and we are all going to have a chance to participate.

The purpose is that ascension is part of our life path and that of everyone on earth today.

But the desire for ascension must be there, which includes the desire and willingness to do the work of healing and transformation to complete it. And we must be willing, despite our fears, to remember the promise and to stand in the purpose of bringing ascension to humanity, the earth, and the universe in a powerful way. Any fear, doubt, or unwillingness we feel around this is a sign of the Atlantean Paradigm which we have to heal in order to complete ascension. The rejection or persecution we experience, whether it's from family, friends, partners or others in our soul group, exists as a reminder that we have invited our Atlantean partners to share in our ascension journey today.

How are the Atlantean Paradigm and its emotional legacy manifesting in your life? Take a closer look at your fears and the emotions you feel around being who you are. Many of you are blessed with extraordinary gifts and yet you hesitate to use them. You don't want to be manipulated or persecuted. You are afraid of being accused, misunderstood or judged. You express your feminine power as the repressed female or your masculine power as the controlling male. You hide your light from others. The challenge that you're faced with now is having the courage to use your gifts and power, without the fear that somehow they will be used against you, humanity and the planet.

If you are a woman today, you may feel used, controlled, manipulated or unsupported by male energy. You may even fear male energy or reject it because of its legacy of power and control. You may experience male energy in your life in the form of abusive, dominating and controlling men.

If you are a man today, you have been conditioned for generations to suppress any aspects of yourself which reflect the feminine, including your emotions. How many boys have heard the expression 'Big boys don't cry'? How many generations of men have been told that in order to be a 'man' you had to deny yourself any emotional expression?

Where do you hold your Atlantean Paradigm energy, what are you afraid of when you think of using your gifts and power? Which of the items below resonate with you?

Being manipulated or taken advantage of by others
Being accused of not telling the truth or of not being right
Seen as someone who is powerful and looked up to by others.
Having a lot of responsibility to or for others.
Being accused of misusing your power.
I will not use my power in the right and best ways.
My life will be out of my control.

Whether you could relate to one or all of the fears listed above, they have to do with how you used your gifts in Atlantis and what you were recognized for. You may have been a brilliant architect, a passionate and powerful teacher, an artist or musician who enriched other's lives. You were a respected leader. Everyone in Atlantis met their needs through instant manifestation. You lived in peaceful, beautiful communities where everyone lived in harmony and abundance.

But it was a society that lacked balance and despite the abundance, peace and your best intentions, there was a dark side that was not only allowed to prevail, you may have been one of those who empowered it. And you may also have helped empower Atlantis' destruction by sharing your power and light for this purpose. Those who misused your power, and that of many others in Atlantis, are probably part of your life today because they are part of the healing of your Atlantean Paradigm.

Who are these people? Name one member of your soul group (which includes your family, friends, partners, children, neighbors) that you feel challenges you by making you uncomfortable in how you use your power and gifts, you feel you cannot be your true self with them, you put yourself or they put you in a victim role, they dominate or control you, or you limit yourself around them.

This soul group partner was one of your antagonists in Atlantis. Or they were someone who lost their life in Atlantis because of your unconscious or conscious participation in its destruction. And your family also plays a role with you in this. What is your relationship with people in your family? Are you one of the group or would people in your family describe you as different, hard to understand or relate to, caring, knowing, patient, or something else?

As you move through these chapters, pay attention to the people who come to your awareness because they are an important part of this soul group connection, which includes commitments you have made, that you will heal and release. There are exercises in later chapters that will help you heal and resolve these connections.

Now let's talk about how you express the Atlantean paradigm in your life, because there are some very unconscious and subtle things you do that impact how you use your power and gifts.

The Atlantis Energy Legacy

Do you describe yourself as someone who doesn't understand technology? Are you afraid of it, does it confuse or intimidate you? Do you wish computers and technology would go away? As a current and former technologist, who is fascinated with technology in all of its aspects, I am surprised at the number of people I know, who are gifted teachers and healers, who are afraid of technology, do not know how to use it or who avoid it entirely. Technology is another interesting aspect of Atlantis because much of the ancient technology we admire, such as the Egyptian pyramids, and Mayan temples and calendar, all originated in Atlantis, which was a very technologically advanced society and culture. They had interstellar transportation, could teleport -- physically travel to other locations by using thought -- and could bi-locate, or be in two places at the same time. There were other ways of moving around and transportation that we can't even begin to imagine today. Some of that technology is being revealed now and there is much more to come.

Those of you who avoid using technology and who call yourselves technologically illiterate and you know who you are, are that way not because you just don't get technology. You have a deep fear of technology as part of your Atlantean experience and paradigm because it was misused to create such destruction, chaos and misery that you've turned yourself off from technology. While you know that it is a useful tool, it can also be a powerful weapon. And maybe that is also because what you see in today's emerging technology is a painful reminder of the technology you remember from Atlantis. Technology is just another way to use energy.

Many of you have become very adept at avoiding technology and managing your life without it or with as little as possible but that is because fear and denial of technology is one way you may deny the existence of the Atlantean paradigm in your life. It is also one way that you deny your

Atlantis energy heritage and all of the power and abilities you had in that lifetime. But it's also one of the ways that you prevent yourself from moving into the next level where you open yourself more and more to your Atlantean gifts because technology, beyond machines, was one of the extraordinary aspects of Atlantis and one of the ways Atlanteans harnessed and utilized energy.

Imagine having the thought "I need to go to the market" and you are at the market. Or "I need to go visit this person" and you are at their front door. Atlanteans could communicate telepathically and be instantly connected to others through their thoughts. Today's cell phone technology, which gives us the ability to instantly contact someone, is a reminder of that technology, as is the internet, which extends our communication ability exponentially. Now we can connect with people we do not know personally, via mediums such as Facebook and Twitter. This was possible in Atlantis without the use of cell phones or computers, in a way that was much more advanced than we have today. The technology was extraordinarily powerful and when you learn how Atlantis was destroyed I think you're going to understand why the fear and unwillingness to use technology is so prevalent among light workers and people who hold the Atlantean paradigm and who specifically came in to heal it.

Those who specifically came in to heal this paradigm have very, very strong connections to their Atlantean memories and their Atlantean roots. You may not be aware of this in your rational mind or thinking, but there is an energetic entire part of you that is very much aware of the connection that you had to Atlantis—the work you did there, the gifts you had and the role you play pre- and post- destruction. You remember both the good and the bad aspects of Atlantis and some of your desire to live in a more utopian environment are from your memory of Atlantis, which was as close as we have ever come to a perfect world. Yet it was not without its flaws, as you will discover. But within your memory there is both a longing for this level of perfection once again and a fear of what may happen if it is resurrected.

The memory you have of your participation in Atlantis can elicit feelings of great sadness as you recall these memories and reconnect with the details that you experienced in a very personal and profound level. Much of these memories are contained within your emotions. How is this emotional energy expressed in your life today? How many of your connections and relationships are full of joy, loving, and empowering?

Emotions are one way we understand and manage energy in the third dimension. They are strongly connected to memory and since our limited brain functioning prevents us from remembering the exact details of our Atlantis experience, we created emotional memories with energetic markers that would remind us of the lessons we had come to experience and change. In the third dimension we experience the world through the five senses-- seeing, hearing, tasting, touching and smelling, which are part of the physical body and we relate to our environment on an emotional level. With our Atlantean Legacy memory stored in our energetic imprint as emotions, we will recall its events when they come to our awareness through our emotions, including fear. And it is by healing these emotional memories and how they present and repeat themselves in our life, that we will heal the Atlantean paradigm and avoid repeating the lessons of Atlantis.

Now that you have read about different aspects of Atlantis and its legacy, you must be asking yourself the bigger question, what really happened? We know that the destruction involved water and believe that Atlantis is buried somewhere under the sea. That's only part of the story and in the next chapter, you will read about the destruction of Atlantis.

The Destruction of Atlantis

What does everyone know about Atlantis? That it fell into the ocean and was destroyed (which is not completely true). Very little is said about its wonderful qualities and attributes although they are its most important aspects. The destruction occurred in spite of Atlantis' advanced culture, knowledge, and technology, not because of it (although there was technology involved in the destruction). Does the mention of Atlantis make you a little teary-eyed, afraid and somewhat reluctant to go there? When you read about the destruction of Atlantis you will know why.

I also want to caution you that in different lifetimes you have expressed many different types and aspects of energy. Some of you may realize that you have been what I'm going to call the villains of this story. In every experience, no matter how important or critical it is on any level, someone has to play the role of the dark side. Contrary to what you may think, it is the most powerful teachers, those capable of the greatest love, committed to creating the most powerful, transformational, healing and motivating learning opportunities, who agree to play this role. Light and dark must be present because it is the dark that allows the light to shine more brightly.

Here's an example given to me by my guide, Archangel Uriel, that I had never thought about before. I had been going through some rather challenging months and was asking why I had chosen to have this experience. One afternoon he told me to go outside and look at the sky on a bright, sunny day. He asked me whether I saw any stars in the sky and I said "Of course not, it's daytime and they don't shine during the day." Uriel gently reminded me that the stars were still shining but I couldn't see them because the light was too bright. Their brilliance could only be seen when the sky was dark.

A balance of light and dark must be present in all situations. So the dark—maybe we will call them the lower vibration or the antagonist—gives the protagonists something to work towards. If ascension wasn't part of this cosmic journey we would be floating among the clouds right now but that's not how the physical universe works. We are an integral part of cycles of destruction and creation, which includes light and dark. Darkness makes the light shine brighter and bear that in mind as you are reading this story because the darkness gives us a chance to shine our light more brightly, and allows for more of our light to be seen.

When we light up the darkness is when our light shines the brightest. Imagine lighting a candle in a dark room and all you see is the light glowing from the candle. Now imagine lighting the same candle in a room that's flooded with light. You won't notice the candlelight because the room is too bright Darkness and light will balance each other out, and in time, balance is always the end result. If you discover your role in Atlantis was dark, then your role today may be that of the light. Whatever darkness you were responsible for in one lifetime is balanced by an equal or greater amount of light in the next. You may have been the architect of Atlantis' destruction and today, you will be the architect of the fulfillment of this ascension cycle.

Atlantis was what we would call heaven on Earth. It was beautiful, the Earth was beautiful, and there was complete harmony with nature. The people had what we would consider to be extraordinary abilities but which were part of their everyday lives. They could teleport, bi-locate, and tele-communicate. They were very aware of their connection to each other, to the Universe and also very aware of energy. Manifestation was how they fulfilled their needs and everyone could instantly manifest whatever they wanted. They knew themselves as part of a universal society and had contact with life forms, energies and beings from other planets, other universes and there was no separation between the material and spiritual worlds. It was all one world. The veil between heaven and earth did not exist. Atlanteans also knew that they were ending an ascension cycle, that they were part of an energetic continuum in the universe, and were well aware of the role they placed in the galactic and universal ascension process.

The people in Atlantis had a specific purpose, everyone had wonderful gifts, and that is how they contributed to and operated in society. There were teachers, architects, cooks, gardeners, doctors, artists, and musicians. Everyone received according to their needs, there was equality, fairness, and sharing. No one took more than they needed because everyone's needs were met according to their desires. If they wanted something, it was instantly available to them because they knew how to use their intention to manifest. There was a strong sense of community and belonging, and there was no war or fighting or greed or corruption.

But that was not all that was happening in Atlantis. In order to overcome the chaos and separation of the Lemurian cycle, it was decided, at the beginning of the Atlantis ascension cycle, that the predominant energy would be feminine so the world could know the loving, gentle, nurturing and supportive energy of the feminine. And since the Earth also had a strong feminine energy, it was thought that this would complement and support the Earth's energy through its ascension process.

But this was the feminine energy as expressed through the ego and it quickly went from dominant to domineering; from being in control to controlling. Men were subservient, repressed, oppressed and powerless. The male energy was denied any substantial participation in Atlantis, except to the extent allowed by women. It was very unbalanced and over time, men began to resent the limitations imposed on them. With no participation in society and little input into its governance, they felt excluded and through this, decided that they would embark on their own ascension journey and work around the women since they were not being included in their decisions or plans.

As the men began to create a separate plan for ascension, they approached the women to get their assistance and input. A compromise was reached and the two groups decided to move forward together but they were still both operating from the ego and distrustful of each other as significant damage had been done to their relationships. There was strong resentment and fear on both sides, which were ignoring one of the main purposes of their Atlantis cycle, which was to bring the masculine and feminine energies into alignment and balance.

While the compromise was intended to promote the sharing of light and energy, to create peace between the male and female energy and participate in the ascension together, the plans put in place still reflected the control that each side insisted on having. And within this desire for control, a group of people, mostly men with a few women, decided that they were going to take over the ascension process and manipulate it for their own purposes. Instead of allowing it to occur naturally, and within the fear of continuing the female dominated society they were repressed in, they wanted to accelerate the process, control the outcome, and use the massive frequencies of light and energy that were being generated in ascension to dominate the Earth and the universe.

The technology they created was similar to what we know today as HAARP (High Frequency Active Aural Research Program), which is used for weather and climate control through concentrating energy and sending high frequency signals into the atmosphere. The purpose of this technology in Atlantis was to raise the energy and vibration of the earth, exponentially multiplying the energy that was already being created through the transformation of the Earth and of humanity. They wanted to make it happen outside the natural ascension path so they could place the Earth at the head of the Universe, so to speak, and not have to be part of the galactic or Universal ascension cycle. The acceleration of ascension, they believed, would make the Earth more powerful, with a greater frequency and of a higher vibration, to control the multi-dimensional aspects of ascension. The concept was to achieve divinity without connecting to and integrating the divine energy.

The technology they created would allow them to harness the energy and light frequencies as they were being raised during the process of empowering the final phases of the ascension cycle. They would collect energy from the people of Atlantis, and concentrate it exponentially by harnessing the energy of the Sun, the brightest and most powerful light in the solar system. Along with the energy, they also wanted to capture the light that people held, concentrating it into a powerful beam that they would use to raise the Earth's frequency and propel it into higher dimensions of being, through multiple dimensions of space. This would avoid, they thought, the slower process of allowing ascension to occur at its own pace and in balance with the rest of the solar system, galaxy and universe.

The plan was to shoot the beam of concentrated energy and light at the Sun, use the Sun's energy to further enhance it and send the beam back to the Earth. The concentrated beam of light and energy, highly magnified by the Sun's energy, would raise the earth's vibration so much that it could jump dimensions and universes, bypassing the other planets in the ascension cycle, putting the earth in its own universe and well out of the energy of future ascension cycles.

The next step was to convince those whose power and light they needed to participate in the plan. This included many of you today, as you were the architects, scientists and healers, teachers, and spiritual leaders in the Atlantean community. While they were told that they were sharing their light and power and helping with the ascension cycle, this was not the truth. But because they trusted each other and thought that everyone had the same intention for ascension, they agreed to participate.

Why did they not see the truth behind this plan? There had been a shift in the nature of society and some were becoming aware of the imbalance between the male and female energy. There was a desire to change this but it was motivated by guilt rather than a higher energy of compassion. The plan was agreed to by a desire to atone for the previous actions and so they did not question the planners' motives. Instead, they agreed to fully participate and help create the technology. And because the dominant energies were more supportive and nurturing, even with the ego's overlay, there was little reason to suspect ulterior motives or power agendas.

The plan sounded good in theory and it may have worked, except for a few miscalculations. The earth's vibrational field was not high enough to withstand the full force of this concentrated energy. As we experience with energy downloads today, energy has to be integrated into the earth's grid and the earth aligned with the new energy's vibrations, which happens gradually, in order for it to be able to withstand the increased levels of energy and radiation. Because this ascension path was creating new frequencies and energies never before experienced on the Earth, they couldn't be aware of or consider that the light they were going to use was much too powerful for the earth to absorb without creating a harmful or dangerous situation.

Their great ideas were driven by an agenda of power and control and ignored the fact that ascension can't be hurried. It is an energetic process whose power is regulated by the delicate balance of light and energy on the Earth and within each of its inhabitants... And it is a process of integration and alignment and occurs in steps or stages. It cannot be controlled by throwing in random amounts of light and energy to arrive at a specific vibration which we think is required for ascension.

To convince Atlantis' population of their good intentions, they told them that this was an experiment whose purpose was to ensure ascension, reminding them of the previous ascension cycle outcomes of Pangea and Lemuria. The message was that this would make ascension better, easier, more aligned with the universal intention, that it would help people and create a better Earth, and help the galactic community.

And the people of Atlantis believed them, partly because they wanted to participate in the hope that it would resolve the imbalance of the male and female energy, and those who supported it were respected and loved leaders and neighbors. And since ascension was a shared focus, anything that would ensure this transition and transformation was embraced by the people of Atlantis, who were committed to the success of this ascension cycle.

There was betrayal at the heart of this plan. The messages that spoke of sharing power to enhance ascension were partly true. But the project's planners said one thing and did another. They told the population, 'We need your power and energy to help with this ascension process. Set your intention to send light and power to this technology so we can concentrate the energy you are using for ascension and assist the process." Capturing the energy and light did not involve hooking people up to a machine or having them participate in a physical process. With their high level of brain functioning, Atlanteans could simply set an intention for the energy and light transfer to the technology and it would happen, as they had a masterful knowledge of energy and how to use it. And we, as Atlantean citizens, participated willingly and joyfully, thinking that we were joining together to empower a very beneficial, helpful, wonderful project that was going to help everyone.

Many of you, as the citizens of Atlantis, not only empowered this technology, which I will call an 'ascension engine', you helped create, design, and build it. You made sure it worked and joyfully participated in the process. And you promoted it to others as a wonderful idea, a great project that would help everyone and would be beneficial to all of humanity, the earth and our galactic community. As you were sending your power and light to this ascension engine, you were also convincing others to do so as well, people who loved and trusted you, who knew you as their teacher, leader, and friend.

But not everyone in Atlantis thought this was a great idea and there was a group of dissenters who tried to call attention to what they suspected was the true nature of this plan. They felt there was not enough information, that the plan was not fully thought out, that there were other motives, besides ascension, at work. They wondered why it was necessary to create technology to enhance the ascension cycle and why it was necessary to harness others' light and energy to make it work.

While they were right, they were not able to convince many people of their suspicions. They were denounced, ridiculed and pilloried by those who were in favor of it, who had once been their friends and fellow teachers. This caused a great division in Atlantis and polarized the community between those who were in favor of and those who were opposed to this plan. And for the first time there were 'outsiders', people who were rejected and persecuted for their beliefs. Some of these dissenters were imprisoned, cast away, and silenced. A few were asked to leave the community. They were heartbroken by this treatment and knew that there was nothing they could do, whatever was about to happen was going to change the path of the ascension cycle.

Some of you belong to this group of dissenters, those who suspected the motives of the planners and who did their best to warn people of what was really happening. You were heartbroken at how you were treated and surprised at the ridicule and rejection you received. This had never happened in Atlantis before and now, at such an important time, all of the wisdom, truth, and knowledge you had been known and respected for, all of the work you had done on behalf of ascension, Atlantis and its people, was completely disregarded. You were outcasts in your own communities and there was nothing you could do to stop what was happening. Those among you who were powerful mystics knew that this was the end of the cycle and it would not end as you had hoped. You also knew that there would be great destruction and suffering, but you had no idea of the extent to which it would happen. So you accepted the rejection and ridicule, stopped sharing this information and speaking out against the plan, and did your best to prepare for what was to come.

The day came when the machine, the 'ascension engine', was to be started. There was a great celebration and much anticipation that everything was going to work out so well. Nothing happened in the first hours and days after the machine was started. Life went on as normal and the machine hummed away, sending beams of concentrated light and energy to the Sun. For the first few days, everyone thought that things were proceeding normally. But the distance from the earth to the Sun is great and the light beam was also programmed to remain on the Sun for a specific period of time and harness its energy before returning to Earth.

After three or four days, the magnified and concentrated energy beam started to come back to the Earth and the result was not what had been anticipated. Atlanteans began to develop the signs and symptoms of what could be called radiation poisoning. Their internal organs and skin burned, they became very sick and began to die in great numbers. The intense radiation burned the vegetation and it died. Birds fell from the sky, animals dropped dead in place, and the water in the lakes and seas began to boil. From deep within the earth they could hear strange sounds and rumblings that lasted all day and night. The earth began to tremble and then to shake, and there were constant earthquakes.

There was an attempt to turn off the 'ascension engine' but even if those who controlled it had allowed it, it was too late. The experiment was called a success, they had been able to harness the energy and light of the people, send it to the Sun, concentrate it and bring it back to the Earth. Those who were unable to withstand the effects of the radiation were obviously not ready for ascension. This was proof of the need for their project and it meant that only those who were the most worthy, deserving, and ready would be part of the Atlantean community in the final hours of ascension.

As the effects of the light beam worsened the people of Atlantis put out a call for help to their galactic neighbors, who came to the Earth to see what was happening. As soon as they saw the beam of light traveling from the Sun to the Earth, they knew that something had been done but they were powerless to stop it. And as they were gathered above the earth, considering what they could do and preparing to evacuate the people of

Atlantis, the unthinkable happened. The Earth rose up and with a mighty shudder, rolled over on its side.

As the galactic community watched, the water of the seas covered Atlantis in a mighty wave. Nothing could escape their path and even if they could, there was nowhere to go. What was once dry land was covered under miles of ocean and sea water. And what had been ocean and sea was now dry land. A few people were rescued by the galactic ships but that number was tiny in comparison with those who perished. The anguish and shock of what had happened reverberated throughout the universe. The sadness and grief over the loss of Atlantis and its people was felt near and far. And the knowledge that without Atlantis, the ascension cycle was over and there would be no access to higher dimensions now resonated throughout the many universes and by its communities who were impacted by this tragic event.

On the Earth, all was still. There was no movement, other than the quiet motion of the waves that now covered the land. Some of the fish in the sea had survived, as had a few animals and birds. The new land would one day be covered with vegetation and there would be people on the Earth again but for now, the Earth was barren of human life.

An ascension cycle had ended and a new one was ready to begin.

The Aftermath and The New Cycle

What had happened? How had this beam of light created the polar shift, in which the earth rotated ninety degrees on its axis? The Earth was not prepared to receive such a massive influx of energy and could not withstand the pressure on its energetic fields. Rather than expanding the Earth's energetic grid and raising its energetic vibration, the intense energy of the light beam fractured the Earth's energetic grid, disrupted its frequency and interrupted the energetic flow that maintains the balance of the Earth's energy and motion. The promise of ascension that Atlantis thought was going to happen ended up being its destruction.

The outcome of the Atlantean cycle was the destruction of the people, technology and lifestyle of Atlantis. A shock wave reverberated throughout the galactic community, many of whom had heard Atlantis' call for assistance but were powerless to help. Those who saw the destruction and annihilation of Atlantis' communities were traumatized although they knew that the polar shift happened so quickly that there was no way to warn people and if they had, there was nowhere for them to go.

And it created the Atlantean Paradigm, the energetic imprint we have today, which is the legacy we bring into the new ascension cycle. We have a vague reminder of the wonderful gifts and abilities that we once had, as well as the reminder of how easily they can be manipulated and abused. Is it possible that our reluctance to use our power today has its origins in our memory of the abuse of power in Atlantis? What we remember of Atlantis is not the beauty, community, wisdom, and peace but the tremendous guilt that we have embodied because of our participation or the tremendous betrayal that we felt, depending on which side we were on, from the destruction of our beautiful planet and the eradication of our dream of ascension. And yet, within the energetic flow of life, as the old cycle was ending, the parameters for the new one were being set.

As we enter the final stages of another ascension cycle, we are once again facing challenges in the form of agendas of power and control. Are you disturbed by what you see in the world today, the collusion between corporations and governments, the rising imbalance between rich and poor, the exploitation, concentration of power and money, weapons of mass destruction, the rise and power of technology, and the fear that is being created to control people?

These things disturb you because at the level of your emotional DNA and cellular memory you see strong parallels between what's happening on the planet and your uncomfortable experience in Atlantis. It is activating your Atlantean Paradigm which it is supposed to do. The foundation of each ascension cycle is built upon the lessons of the previous ones. Healing precedes transformation and the rise of these memories represent powerful healing opportunities for all of humanity as we move beyond Atlantis and its legacy to complete the work that we did not finish them.

Now that we know what happened in Atlantis and you have an idea of what has been holding you back or limiting you in your life, because of your embodiment of the Atlantean Paradigm, it is time to take the next step, which is to allow this to heal and expand your energetic vibration to allow our current ascension cycle to move forward.

To understand the healing aspects of this journey, let's look at the parameters that were created for our current ascension cycle. You will see that these parameters are the foundation of our social, political, religious, government and corporate systems today.

The first parameter involved the masculine and feminine energy balance. It was clear that the dominant feminine was not the best solution because the feminine energy did not possess the drive and action orientation that were necessary to create the power connections required to keep the ascension energy moving. And this energy, integrated in the ego, became controlling and exclusionary, not fulfilling the purpose of integrating the masculine/feminine energies in their divine aspects. So in the next cycle the masculine energy was allowed to dominate, with the purpose of keeping the energy flowing, creating balance within the masculine and feminine, and integrating their divine aspects to create the ego/divine partnership.

The next parameter involved awareness of energy, gifts and talents. Atlanteans were very aware of their gifts and talents and masters at using energy. But this made them lazy, complacent, and they lost their focus and let themselves be used by their energy instead of using it. So in the next ascension cycle, awareness of energy would arrive through a process of awakening and would follow an intentional desire to embrace energetic potential. The same held true for the gifts, talents and abilities, including their intuition, telepathy and transport. In the new ascension cycle, these would be limited until the people were able to attain the vibrational frequencies where they could appreciate their benefits and use them with conscious intention.

A parameter was created to limit intergalactic awareness, contact, and communication until the collective energy was high enough to accept the responsibility of active membership within the galactic community. And the galactic community wanted to ensure that ascension was achieved by overcoming the third dimensional energies and the balanced use of free will, integrated with the divine energies that would prevent another Atlantis-like cataclysm. Within this parameter, the Earth was isolated from the galactic community and would be unaware of its presence. The galactic community could monitor the Earth's progress, but they would be hidden from view. And the true nature of the other planets in the solar system, galaxy and universe would also be invisible to everyone on Earth until they were ready to access this level of connection.

With Atlantis, there had been a blurring of the dimensions so that within the third dimension it was possible to experience aspects of being in higher dimensions, such as enhanced intuition and the use of energy. A parameter was created to remove this access so the third dimension experience would be limited to the five physical senses and the collective of humanity would have to achieve the vibrational frequency necessary to activate their extra-sensory abilities and access other dimensions.

The use of the 'ascension machine' was Atlantis' way of proving its superiority to the divine, an attempt to reach the status of divinity without the integration of or alignment with Source. A new parameter for the ascension cycle was the introduction of religion, the experience of man as God, which would be their understanding of divinity until humanity could acknowledge its Source connection, accept its divine aspects, and achieve the humility and surrender required to balance the ego with the divine.

The polarity of the second dimension would be established as the dominant energy flow of the Earth until humanity could achieve awareness of its power and learn how to manage the intentional use of power for higher purposes. Separation would exist until humanity chose connection. Dark would exist as a powerful energy, balanced by the light that could be chosen by humanity but in accordance with the level of their vibrational frequency.

The Earth would no longer support humanity in the same way it was supported in Atlantis. Until humanity could love, honor and respect the Earth, the relationship between humanity and the Earth would be one of separation and challenge. The Earth would fully embody third dimensional energies and present an environment that was both beautiful and fearsome, hostile and inviting, until humanity could learn to work with the Earth and honor its participation on the ascension path.

And humanity would have to know fear, pain, and suffering until it learned to create and choose higher frequencies for its experiences.

These new parameters set the foundation for the Earth's new ascension cycle, the one we are experiencing today. While it may appear that humanity was being punished for what it did in Atlantis, the opposite is true. All of the misuses of energy that were experienced created karma, or an energetic imprint within the Earth's vibrational field, that had to be healed. This healing is similar to the karmic healing that we do in lifetimes and karma can only be healed by its creator. So the collective karma that was created in Atlantis was part of the new ascension cycle and its healing had to be completed by humanity, individually and collectively, as part of the ascension journey.

The greater lessons of Atlantis, which we are experiencing today, are lessons in power, connection, and in the balance of the masculine and feminine energies. After the unbalanced female energies of Atlantis, it was decided that the male energy would be dominant and so it has been in this ascension cycle. But we have come full circle, the feminine energy is rising again and we are at the crossroads of another ascension cycle, where we will achieve completion if we can learn to balance these energies and find ways to be powerful within the shared aspects of both masculine and feminine.

Who and what we give our power to, and how we do or do not acknowledge our power are all part of the Atlantean Paradigm. In many ways, modern Earth mirrors Atlantis and as we come ever closer to the ascension crossroads, the choices we make today will determine how the ascension cycle will be completed. We are all surrounded by demands for our power, from the relentless 'buy me' messages we receive from retailers, to politicians who woo our votes, to governments that pass laws which limit our behavior and fine us heavily for noncompliance, to corporations that control how we live, spend money, how much we have to spend, and how we get through our day.

It's a classic example of the Ponzi scheme, something which has made the headlines many times in the past few years in part, to bring this aspect of Atlantis back to our awareness. What is a Ponzi scheme? It is a promise of fantastic returns if you give someone your money. Investors don't realize that a steady stream of new investors makes it possible to pay the old ones. Eventually the Ponzi scheme collapses under its own weight. That is how Atlantis fell, there was a promise of extraordinary return in exchange for the contribution of energy and power (money is a measure of value and energy in the third dimension).What makes Ponzi schemes so attractive is their promise that they can do for others what they do not think they can do for themselves. And people give their power away to others because they believe that they know and can do more than they can.

We will avoid the Ponzi scheme mentality by creating a power base within ourselves, awakening our pre-destruction Atlantean gifts and talents, creating balance between the male and female energies, and fulfilling the terms of the other parameters that were set for this ascension cycle. Then we must use those energies to ascend into the new earth in a peaceful, graceful way that blesses the Earth, humanity, our galactic communities and the universe, to fulfill the promise of ascension into higher dimensions of being.

We cannot accelerate ascension except through the intentional desire for healing and transformation that must come from within each of us. Aside from healing our Atlantean Paradigm and the Atlantis Legacy that we all share, we must maintain our focus on what we want for this ascension cycle, whose purpose is to move us into our divinity

It was believed and shared that a bigger, better, more powerful Earth would be created with the technology assisted ascension but it was lacking the most critical elements, the balance, benefit, and participation of the higher frequencies of spirit and the integration of and alignment with these higher frequencies. The process was the equivalent of creating heaven on Earth, the purpose of the Atlantean ascension cycle, without the benefit of spirit or a true ascension into high vibrations. It would be done from the outside in, from the ego, rather than from the inside out, which is how transformation with spiritual or higher frequency energies occurs.

One thing the creators of this technology did not understand or consider is that it is the collaborative participation in ascension of all of the Earth's people that makes it possible. The combined frequencies of all of the participants is what creates the shift in the Earth's electromagnetic field, raises its vibrations, and creates the potential for ascension to occur . It is not possible to manipulate this process without creating an imbalance that will contribute to some kind of disaster. Unfortunately, the lessons of

Pangea and Lemuria were not fully learned, and were going to be experienced again so their energies were included in the Atlantean Paradigm.

Was Atlantis a promise broken or was it a promise kept? It depends on how you look at it, although it was neither. The fact that ascension didn't happen wasn't a broken promise, we were not ready to access the higher levels of vibration because if we were, it would have happened with Atlantis and we would be living in a much different world today. Another aspect of Atlantis that contributed to its demise was that there was too much of everything. People were too comfortable, too connected, there was no reason for them to work hard at anything, and they became complacent. It's similar to the concept of someone having everything they want, what goals, dreams or desires can they have? Have we, as a collective population, been lulled into complacency with too much stuff, the lure of having more, being better than everyone else, of focusing our energy on things outside of ourselves?

While there was a collective intention for ascension, it was not accompanied by a true desire to have this happen. Atlanteans thought that ascension would come just as easily as everything else in their lives did. Although they were very committed to it, they didn't have a compelling need for it because their lives were already wonderful, easy and fulfilling. There wasn't enough of a difference between the way their lives were and what the promise of ascension held for them. This is one of the reasons we were born with such limited functioning and limited capacity to use our power and intellect as humans today, and one of the reasons that suffering is embodied in the human experience, to compel us to choose ascension because the other path, not ascending, as not as pleasant. Unless we, as humans, have something to work towards, we are easily distracted by Ponzi schemes that promise us great returns for our minimal investment of our time, energy and power.

Before we look at your Atlantean Legacy, let's consider the areas in which you embody it. This is an energetic imprint so it is expressed in all areas of your life through how you use your power, gifts, and intention.

Atlantis' destruction was caused by the misuse of power. One aspect of the Atlantean Paradigm impacts how we view and use our power. We entered this lifetime with an awareness of how destructive the abuse of power and energy can be. And there are two ways to resolve this, one way is we give our power away to people and hope they won't misuse it or abuse it.

The other way is we pretend we don't have any power so there's nothing to give away or to be taken advantage of. If we don't acknowledge that we have power we are not responsible for anything because we can't participate without power. So we live our lives as very powerless people and hope that others will 'do the right thing' or not abuse their own power, or ours, and harm us in the process.

Within your own life, how do you deal with the issue of power?

Do you give your power away to those you think are powerless or who you believe are more powerful than you are?

Or do you pretend you don't have any power so you don't have to be responsible and live a very powerless life?

The same thing happens with your gifts. In Atlantis we had extraordinary gifts of communication, manifestation, and with the use of energy. The more powerful you were in Atlantis, the more gifts and talents you had, the greater your contribution was to Atlantis' destruction as you willingly volunteered your gifts in an attempt to accelerate ascension. So you may view your gifts as a source of pain and destruction rather than a source of blessing.

Do you use your gifts or deny them?

Are you afraid that someone will take advantage of your gifts or misuse them?

Do you feel guilty in having gifts you think others don't have?

Intention is how we control energy. In Atlantis reality was created through intention as they were masters at working with and controlling energy. But this intention was used to harness the collective light and energy of Atlantis' most powerful teachers, healers and leaders to create the ascension technology. Today we are unaware of how powerfully our intention works and we often use it without regard to its potential. Intention, combined with our gifts and power, is an unstoppable force. So we ignore the power of intention and instead, use hope and trust to create our reality.

How do you use your power of intention to create your reality?

Do you powerfully intend the highest and best outcomes for yourself?

Do you feel guilty when you put your needs first?

Do you believe that you deserve to be powerful and gifted?

How do you intend your reality into being?

A final issue in the Atlantean Paradigm is trust. Within our Atlantean Paradigm we either don't trust anyone or we trust people who will abuse our trust to fulfill their own agenda or who do not know what to do with our trust and the power that accompanies it. And within our Atlantean soul groups that we have gathered today, we are often giving them our trust so they will make different choices for ascension.

Who do you trust with your power and gifts?

Are they worthy of your trust and do they honor this gift?

Do you trust others in the hope that they will 'do the right thing' and not abuse your trust?

Do you trust yourself?

Where do you trust people? The desire to trust others is hidden within your ability to be compassionate and empathic. This is where you are aware of others feelings, limitations, pain and suffering. You know what their hopes and dreams are, especially the ones they are not expressing.

What do you feel compelled to do when you feel someone's pain or suffering, doubt, confusion or fear?

Do you feel compelled to share your power or gifts with them?

Do you want to help them and fix their problems?

Are you afraid that if you do not make their life better that they do something to make your life worse?

This is an aspect of the Atlantean Paradigm that causes us to step in and help others so they do not feel powerless and in doing so, create havoc in the world. Did you find any parallels between these questions and your life today? In the next section we will talk about the Atlantean Guilt, another aspect of the Atlantis Legacy that also controls how you use and share your power. Is it easy for others to make you feel guilty or to shame you? If it is, then guilt and shame are important motivators for you and through them, you have chosen your life path and soul groups and your ascension destiny in this lifetime.

The Atlantean Guilt

If you have problems with guilt and shame or if using your power creates feelings of guilt, you are expressing your Atlantean Paradigm through an aspect that I call the Atlantean Guilt. This is an emotional imprint whose origins lie in the remorse we felt over having destroyed the Earth and in not completing the ascension process for ourselves and the rest of the universe. While we are unaware of our relationship with the greater universal community today, we were very aware of it in Atlantis. We knew, as we destroyed the Earth, that the implications were not limited to what was happening with us, they extended to include all of the beings who were ascending with us, across the many universes.

Within the Atlantean Guilt imprint we empowered the limitations and fear that were introduced in the foundation for this ascension cycle. We also willingly gave our power away to those who we thought would save or prevent us from using it in such unwise and destructive ways. The domination and control which we have known for centuries is how we have punished ourselves for what happened in Atlantis. It is also why we have allowed ourselves to be manipulated by our governments, religions, political institutions and soul groups, to atone for our misuse of power.

But this guilt, as with all guilt, is misguided because it doesn't take into account the many aspects required for ascension. When a cycle is completed, it is fulfilled within the energetic vibrations of those who participate and the effect cannot be greater than the energy the have aligned with and integrated.

Through this guilt we have created the very thing we hoped it would avoid, the use of ego-based energies to control the ascension process. As we hear of the manipulation and control that governments and corporations exert over populations, we are reminded of how we shared our power in Atlantis, to those who told us that they would take care of us and provide the smoothest ascension transition to ascension. If you feel uneasy and uncomfortable with much of what is happening in the world, it is because you are making connections to your Atlantis experience. The more guilt you feel around your power, the more power you had in Atlantis. Is there someone in your life who you feel resents your power and abilities and who appears to have much less than you do? Do you use this guilt to limit yourself, your success, transformation and the use of your power?

This Atlantean Guilt paradigm is also why you do not accept your gifts and talents, or do not allow yourselves to benefit from and share them with others. Through the painful reminder of how you believe you betrayed your students, friends, and family in Atlantis you distrust yourselves and yet, in order to shift the energy in the current cycle, to end the control and prevent a repeat of Atlantis' destruction, this is what you must do. And there is an aspect of deserving and worthiness within this guilt paradigm that prevents you from believing that you are worthy of the re-awakening of the wonderful gifts you had in Atlantis. By judging yourself in this way you are actually limiting your ability to fully participate in ascension and to fully heal the Atlantis cycle so we can complete ascension now and realize our place within the galactic community once again, to complete the journey beyond the third dimension.

The paradigms that were created at the beginning of this cycle, those that limited access to energy, information, and power, were put in place to allow more balanced transformation, so the ego would experience the full effects of its domination to allow and even invite spirit into the third dimension. The damage caused in Atlantis happened because of ego domination, a result of excessive and unbalanced use of the free will energy, which could choose any path of frequency. Without the desire or willingness to choose higher vibrations, which are always present, the ascension process became an undisciplined, unbridled power grab. Can you see anything in the world today that mirrors this? There are many examples of it and yet, there are also many examples of those who are willing to acknowledge and accept their power, who are working hard to educate people about spirit, higher dimensions of being, access to different frequencies, and how to use their gifts and power.

The Atlantean Guilt is being brought forward unconsciously by the governments and corporations whose power and existence have always depended on the willingness of people to give away or share their power. As governments announce they are no long able to provide services to support their populations, or enact policies that tread on freedoms, they are acting within the permissions that our Atlantean Guilt has given them, through their control. At the same time, they are releasing their power and control by refusing to support us.

As corporations reveal their self interests, fire or lay off employees, cut benefits and pay, they are also acting within the permissions that were bestowed under our Atlantean Guilt, through which we ignore, share or give away our power. And they are also simultaneously releasing their power and control by refusing to support us. Those who depend on these services and benefits for their livelihood are angry but it is an invitation to choose to step into their own power, to reclaim their powerful Atlantean heritage, without the legacy of guilt, and become more powerful manifestors in their lives. The message we have always received from those we give our power too, 'We will take care of you,' is very similar to the one that was shared with us so many lifetimes in ago in Atlantis, 'Give us your power and we will use it to make this transition into ascension as smooth as possible.' Everything that is happening in the world today is an invitation for us to reclaim our Atlantean gifts and power and to use them to complete this ascension cycle.

It is time to release the Atlantean Guilt because it prevents us accepting the full range, scope and abilities of our power and how we can use them in the world today. Through it we humble ourselves, by placing ourselves below everything else and every other energy in the universe. Our humility has acted as a wall preventing our direct Source connection. Over many lifetimes this wall has appeared in the form of religions, kings, leaders, and rulers, governments, politicians, and social restrictions. We humble ourselves because we fear arrogance and yet, there is a more balanced placement of these energies, as the co-creator, the divine spirit/human partnership and the reconnection between the human and spirit worlds through higher dimensions of being.

When we empower ourselves, we release the limitations of the Atlantis Legacy and Paradigm and we stop its effects in our lives. Judging ourselves for Atlantis' destruction is one way we have atoned for what we did but there is no place for judgment in higher dimensions, just as there is no place for fear. Can we love ourselves enough, despite how we feel about what happened in Atlantis, to become powerful, limitless, gifted and divine once again? We must because unless we do, we will not complete this cycle with an ascension into higher vibrations of being.

Atlantean Soul Groups

Everything we have done across our many lifetimes in this ascension cycle has been set up to mirror our Atlantean experiences. Each ascension cycle sets the foundation for the next one. To know how your Atlantean Legacy figures into your life you can look at your feelings and beliefs around your power, gifts, energy and intention. Do you have issues around trust, either not trusting others, trusting people who abuse your trust, or being afraid to trust?

This information is available by looking at who you chose as your soul mates and your soul groups. So many of your soul mates, especially the relationships that you are being challenged by right now, are part of your Atlantean Legacy. Within these soul mate relationships you have chosen people who mirror your soul's energy with respect to Atlantis. All of your wounds, memories, cellular and emotional DNA, the pain, guilt and shame, are all present in your soul group dynamics. They hold this energetic space for you, as well as the potential for your healing.

Despite the romantic focus they are often given, soul mates are our teachers. And because our connection with them is at the level of our emotional DNA and cellular memory, they are very powerful teachers. When clients tell me they want a soul mate, I always tell them to think hard about what they are asking for because they will choose a teacher whose lessons they cannot ignore and the experience will change their life in profound ways. By mirroring your soul's energy back to you soul mates carry aspects of your energetic imprint, cellular memory and emotional DNA, which is why the attraction is so powerful and compelling. When you choose a soul mate, you are committing to your healing path.

Our choice of former Atlantean partners as our soul mates in this lifetime was intentional, because this is how we would heal our Atlantean Legacy. In many cases, we chose them from our guilt and shame imprints because we felt guilty about our role in their lives and shamed by our abuse of their trust. Or they were part of the group of Atlanteans who were responsible for the ego-led agenda and we are trying to help them avoid this path and make other choices. We have allowed many of these former Atlantean partners to become the leaders of our government, religious and social institutions today, as part of the larger Atlantis Legacy healing of humanity.

The concept of atonement comes up when we talk about soul mates and soul groups. Atonement means to bring back into wholeness, or at-onement. But we use it through the guilt and shame aspects of our Atlantis Legacy and the overall Atlantean Paradigm, to victimize and martyr ourselves as a display of our remorse, to help others choose a different path. Our belief is if we show them how disempowered their actions make us, we can compel them to use their energy in more powerful and beneficial ways.

There are two different kinds of soul group connections within our Atlantis Legacy. One is through the guilt we have about being responsible for their death and the misuse of our power. We atone by being the victim and martyr, by acknowledging their pain through how we limit our life. We limit our power, gifts and intention so we can show others how sorry we are for what we did.

Does this ring true for you?

Or we chose our soul groups and soul mates through the energetic imprint of our shame. As we acknowledge how we allowed our energy and light to be misused, or that we misused others' power, energy and trust, we want to show them a different path for their energy. By becoming their spiritual teachers we hope they will learn about a higher path and not follow our Atlantean example. But instead of teaching by being powerful, we teach by being ashamed of our gifts and power. By wearing our shame we allow them to punish us, to victimize and martyr us, we remove our boundaries and limits, allowing them free rein in our lives until they give us permission to move on. We can also limit our power, remove our boundaries, let them victimize us and hope that eventually they will be ashamed of their behavior and connect with us in more powerful ways?

Does this resonate with any situation in your life?

And we can choose our Atlantean soul group from both guilt and shame. In this way we become the scapegoat for our Atlantean experience, holding ourselves responsible and accountable for every aspect of Atlantis' destruction, including others' unwillingness or inability to use their free will to make more powerful choices. We have forgotten that they also had choices to make and they unwisely chose to share their power too.

For today's ascension cycle to complete we have to be willing to use our power. Do we dare become powerful again? What are the potential ramifications and outcomes if we do? If we are martyring ourselves in light of our Atlantean memories and energetic imprints because of our gilt and shame over what happened in the past, are we going to repeat the past if we abandon that path? Is it possible for us to create a different outcome now? Then what happens to our soul group and how do they complete their healing?

That's a chance we are going to have to take if we are going to fulfill our lifetime mission of completing this ascension cycle and bring the Earth into higher dimensions of being. Our desire to atone for what we think are our wrongs will have to find a new expression, through the best and highest use of our power, gifts and intention so we can become the light for the new world, instead of a martyr for our past, and light the way of the ascension path.

We must release our fear around the misuse of power even though it is so evident in the world of today. Power is misused by governments and politicians, by corporations and institutions, people suffer and are victimized and yet we can use this information to underscore the danger of having too much power or to remind ourselves that there are many ways to use power. Rather than recalling the memory of how we misused our power in Atlantis, we can use it embrace our power with the intention for ascension and the completion of this cycle in ways we know that it can happen. We are the promise of ascension, so how can you use your power to move yourself, humanity, the earth and the galactic community ever closer to the end?

While we fear that the Earth will be destroyed again, there are advantages that we have today which we did not have in Atlantis. First, the Earth's frequency is much higher now and we know that by the number of electromagnetic storms we are experiencing. With each of the Sun's solar storms and flares vast amounts of energy are sent to the Earth, which raises its energetic frequency. This is helping integrate higher amounts of energy into the Earth's energetic field in a way that is not destructive, in a process that was similar to Atlantis' 'ascension engine' but in a way that is much more natural, controlled and balanced.

Within the context of our limited energetic awareness, we have created a much stronger, more balanced, widespread and higher frequency foundation of collective consciousness. Vast numbers of people are aware of their spiritual heritage, and there is a desire to connect with each other so the ego's domination is being limited to make room for spirit. It is something we have to work at and at times it is hard work. It doesn't always come easy but it is helping us avoid the complacency and lack of motivation that interfered with the Atlantean ascension cycle.

Our spiritual evolution is an energetic spiral and is not linear. As we heal, grow, learn and transform, we move up this spiral into higher dimensions of being. There is an activation which occurs in this process that increases the amount of energy available to us with each step that we rise up the spiral. So while we are still operating in the third dimension, as humans, we are also able to access limited amounts of higher dimensional frequency, overcoming the limitations set up in the Atlantean Paradigm. This is creating a stronger foundation for our eventual permanent entry into higher dimensions and raising the individual frequency to much higher levels.

The Intention for Ascension

What we are doing in ascension now is very important. How much energy are we comfortable with? How much of our power are we willing to express and live with? Where we are on our ascension path and how slowly or quickly we will proceed depends on our willingness to be in our power. This point is different for everyone. My ascension path is different from yours, which is also different from that of everyone you know. We all share a collective journey as part of the Earth's ascension cycle and that of our solar system, galaxy and universe, but each one of us has our own source connection. We have our own ascension cycle. Just as I can't breathe for you and you can't breathe for me, I can't ascend for you; nor can you ascend for me. So yes—we're part of the whole but we also have our own individual path that we have to walk as well.

What's your intention for your ascension? Besides participating in the end of a cycle which, for you, may also be the culmination of many ascension cycles, what is your intention for yourself? It's something we each have to consider because we tend to think of ascension as a future goal for the Earth but it is also part of our lives. We cannot separate the Earth's ascension from ours and work towards making the Earth a better place, the reconnection of humanity to Source, our collective journey into higher dimensions of being without considering what that means to us. Making the Earth a 'better' place is a generic goal for ascension and it doesn't serve us in any way.

As you consider your own intentions for this, consider these questions:

Are you willing to be powerful?

Are you willing to use your gifts to be in your power, to contribute to this cycle in a much more positive and much more powerful way?

Are you willing to shine your light?

What does your ascended life look like?

Intention, or misguided intention, may have brought Atlantis down but it will also complete this ascension cycle and we need to be willing to use this powerful ability for ourselves, as well as for the Earth and humanity, to complete this ascension cycle by opening the pathways into higher dimensions of being.

Integrating the Healing

Profound healing occurs when we connect with a new realization. Sometimes it is a message we have heard many times before and then one day something within us is awakened and it becomes part of our truth. The new realization can either empower us to greater heights or depress us as we realize where we have limited ourselves and how we have used our power in other circumstances and lifetimes. In the first part of this book we talked about the basics, previous ascension cycles, how Atlantis was destroyed, the Atlantean Guilt, the Atlantean Paradigm and Legacy, and the limitations that were placed on us at the beginning of this ascension cycle. This was not a punishment for our wrongdoing, although it can feel that way. Instead, it was a way of ensuring that our use of power was balanced with spirit, that the ego would eventually find reasons for and safety in creating a human/spirit partnership. This is what would allow ascension to occur and it would happen when we were ready for it and willing to choose it from a point of power, surrender, humility and grace.

An ascension cycle is a process of shifting energetically into higher vibrations and we do that by moving through different dimensions. The Earth has also risen through dimensions, beginning with only darkness in the first dimension, adding light and chaos created the second dimension. Emotional energy, intention, and free will created the third dimension we live in today.

Through this we also had other ascension cycles, with Pangea, Lemuria and Atlantis. These ascension cycles moved us into higher dimensions of being but were limited by the level of energetic frequency held by the Earth and humanity. Within our current ascension cycle we are integrating spirit and becoming more divine, actualized, and moving towards the incarnation of ourselves as spiritual humans. Instead of being led by our emotions we begin to take into account things like responsibility and understanding our power and realizing that we have the obligation to use it.

We call this process of movement earth cycles but they have a larger influence because we are part of a universal ascension cycle. All of the planets in our solar system have completed their own ascension, which we also participated in, and we are the last planet to complete ascension. Once we do, our solar system, galaxy, universe and many other universes complete a much larger ascension cycle. Then the ascension cycles are repeated at different levels and within different dimensions. It is important to not focus on the end because there is no true 'end', there are only completions that allow for new cycles to begin.

We have all been part of many different ascension cycles but the last three are the ones that have special significance to our current cycle. One thing that Pangea, Lemuria and Atlantis share in common is that they are all third dimension ascension cycles and represent movement within the third dimension to prepare us for an eventual movement into higher dimensions of being.

In the Pangaean cycle the moon broke off of the Earth and we had the separation of the heart and mind. In Lemuria the single land mass broke up into seven continents and this was the separation of humanity into different tribes and cultures. With this we separated ourselves from Source.

With Atlantis, our most recent ascension cycle, the Earth experienced a polar shift in which the Earth flipped on its side due to Atlantean manipulation of the ascension energy. With this shift, everything that was once underwater was now dry land and what had been dry land was now underwater. It is interesting to note here that all of the world's major religious teachings refer to some kind of flooding event or great inundation. In the Bible it was Noah's ark. This refers to the end of the Atlantis ascension cycle and what we know as 'modern' history begins at that point.

The story of Atlantis was the desire to create heaven on Earth without the divine aspects, to make humanity larger than God. And if you remember in the biblical story, the Tower of Babel, how humanity got together to reach the heavens and show humanity's superiority, that's the story of Atlantis. In fact, it's the story of every ascension cycle in the third dimension.

The emotional and cellular imprint of Atlantis destruction is what we call the Atlantean Legacy. It affects how we use our energy and more specifically, the fear around using our energy, power and gifts. Since we were manipulated into sharing our energy in ways that caused Atlantis' destruction, we have come into this lifetime with a profound fear of being powerful. And yet, in order to complete this ascension cycle, we must be willing to use our power and gifts without the fear that they will be abused or manipulated.

The Atlantean Paradigm is the set of parameters that were created as the foundation for our current ascension cycle. They determine the balance of masculine and feminine power, our access to our gifts, talents, intuition and power, our relationship with the Earth, the role that pain and suffering play in our life paths that also involve karma. And our access to higher dimensions and the galactic community was removed until we could be at an energetic frequency and vibration to use this level of connection more responsibly.

We also share an Atlantean Guilt imprint that has impacted how we limit the use of our gifts and power. It has also contributed to our choice of soul group partners and how we interact with them. Through our guilt we see ourselves as unworthy, undeserving, and obligated to atone for our role in the destruction of Atlantis, its community, and the Earth. We do this by martyring and victimizing ourselves within our soul group, helping them find their power by relinquishing ours or giving it away.

Our fear and mistrust of technology has strong Atlantean roots, as Atlantis was a very technologically advanced society and it was destroyed through the misuse of technology. Before we move into the clearing and healing work, let's set the stage by remembering Atlantis as it was, a paradise on earth. It was beautiful, peaceful and loving. We were powerful, with full use of our brain functioning, all of our DNA was active. We created our reality solely through manifestation. Atlantis was the pinnacle of human evolution.

Then we shared our light and energy to empower the completion of our ascension cycle with a group whose agenda was ego-led. Motivated by power and driven by the desire to create heaven on earth without the participation of spirit, they built technology that would capture the light and energy of Atlantis' people, concentrate it by sending it to the Sun and on its return to Earth it would raise the earth's vibrations and jump start the ascension process. Instead, the Earth shifted on its axis, destroying Atlantis and all of humanity.

This is where we are today, nearing the completion of another ascension cycle and much of what is happening today sounds very much like what happened in Atlantis just before its destruction. Does this scare you? It is rather scary because we remember Atlantis' disastrous results that came about because of the misuse of power, the manipulation of energy, and personal agendas motivated by a desire for power and control.

Each ascension cycle creates the foundation for the next one and to change the results of the Atlantean ascension we had to get ourselves to the point where those decisions were made. And we are there now, with many of the same details in place including secret groups with hidden agendas and a desire to rule the world. Our response to their plots has been to resist using our power so they won't have access to it. We think that we are preventing them from doing their dastardly deeds when all we're doing is not allowing ourselves to be fully in our power. This tactic also denies us the power that we need to empower this ascension cycle to its full completion.

What exists in the world community is also reflected in our own lives. Is there someone in your life who you feel uses or abuses your power? Are you feeling manipulated by their agenda? Are you afraid to use or acknowledge your power and gifts? It's time to embrace our full power, gifts, energy and potential for ascension.

Every ascension cycle reaches a point of promise where the result can go either way. We are at that point now. And it can go either way for us too. Remember that ascension is a potential but it's not guaranteed. We are the fulfillment of ascension and it is what we do that creates the final outcome. What have we done to help this process along?

We have worked hard to rise to new levels of soul growth.

We have healed our karmic cycles and worked through many lifetimes of karma.

We have achieved new levels of emotional learning, using it to empower our spiritual growth.

We have been willing to heal, learn, grow and transform on every level.

And we are fully committed to this ascension cycle.

We have also put ourselves back into the energy of Atlantis where we are re-experiencing our memories, realizations and fears. Atlantis was destroyed when humanity, based on the actions and agenda of a small group but with the participation of a much larger community, tried to become God-like without the benefit of spirit, to create a superior Earth instead of the heaven/earth partnership that is the purpose of ascension.

Today's ascension cycle is divine, which is acknowledging the divine within us and within all things, and creating the 'spiritual human' with an ego/divine partnership. What we must avoid, as our Atlantis memories return, is to think that it is hopeless, that as individuals we are powerless and have no impact on the outcome. While it's a collective journey, each of us empowers the collective in an exponential way so our participation is essential to the outcome we want to create. We need to go beyond the fear of repeating Atlantis and create a different outcome that fulfills the promise of ascending into higher dimensions of being. We are much closer to that end that you may believe.

How do we empower ascension? By not repeating what we did to destroy Atlantis.

We destroyed Atlantis by not appreciating the full potential of our gifts and allowing them to be used and misused by others.

We destroyed Atlantis by not fully appreciating the value and use of our power and allowing it to be used and misused by others.

We destroyed Atlantis by not understanding the power of our intention and allowing it to be used and misused by others.

We destroyed Atlantis by believing that it could be facilitated and completed by others on our behalf, that we were not capable of ensuring its success.

And we will connect to our inner guidance, developing our self trust so we align ourselves with people we can trust, and who are trustworthy, beginning with trusting ourselves.

We will complete this ascension cycle by valuing and appreciating our power, gifts and intention and using them in a conscious and intentional way, to move ourselves and the Earth through the end of the third dimensional experience and into higher dimensions of being.

One of the Atlantean Paradigm aspects we will be clearing is the soul group connection as many of our soul group members are our Atlantean partners. And we have taken on the responsibility for their healing by living through our Atlantean Guilt and shame with them. We have opened our hearts, spirit, power and energy to them and invited them into a shared path with us so that we could atone for what we've done. But we resolve our past guilt by overcompensating in the present, trying to make up for destroying the Earth and their lives by creating an artificial support system for them now. It's very self-destructive and limiting path which blocks our ascension path and theirs.

In this divinity ascension cycle, we must learn to incorporate the divine without destroying the ego. It isn't an either/or choice, it's the creation of a human/divine partnership. This was central to the Atlantean ascension cycle. The ego-based thinking that our divinity would overrule and control our humanity and life path manipulated our intention and how we used our power. Yet from within the fear of losing our power was born the reality we feared the most, the tragic end of Atlantis. From our fear of relinquishing our power to Source, we gave it away voluntarily to a group that was going to use it for their own purposes and make us truly powerless. In fearing the loss of power we invited it chaos and destruction into our lives.

As we feel the energy building in intensity, we have to take action, not through doing, by 'being' our most powerful, gifted, talented, willing, enlightened, spirit-filled, determined, and committed selves. We have been those things for decades and perhaps even lifetimes but often in isolation and silence, working quietly from the sidelines and in the background, supporting the energy that we knew would one day prevail.

Now it's time for us to emerge from our isolation. We have been isolated from the world and from each other for a very long time, partly because of our own fears, partly because there was a lot of healing we needed to do. The healing work is now nearly completed and we need to take healing's second step (the healing work is the first step), which is to take action. This can be a scary step for us because it does involve getting 'out there', taking back our mantle of power and moving energy in ways that may remind us of Atlantis' experience. But our only other choice is to do nothing and we know that is not a good choice because without our participation, and that means each one of us, we greatly limit our ability to complete this cycle in the way we know it can be done.

Before you judge yourself for not doing this sooner, remember that healing begins when we choose to acknowledge and accept our power. And that is a big choice, given the Atlantean Guilt and other imprints that are in place, individually and collectively. It is a choice that is made in the moment when we are ready to shift our own Atlantis Legacy and release the Atlantean Guilt. It is not a choice that could have been made a week, year, or a decade ago and it coincides with where we are in the ascension cycle, individually and collectively.

Everything we have done until this moment was part of our own Atlantis energetic imprint so we could heal the aspects we embodied. Whether you have spent your time raising children, working at a corporate job, flying planes, or digging ditches, the time to begin is when you choose to acknowledge and accept your power. Which also means that it's time, in this ascension cycle, to release our Atlantis Legacy and move into the next stages of this cycle.

Are you ready to step out of the physical, mental, emotional, and spiritual isolation you have been in for so long?

Are you ready to accept your mantle of power and join your Earth and galactic community to complete this cycle?

Are you ready to create a new, human/spirit partnership for heaven on earth, to move into higher dimensions of being now?

I know you are and I am too, so let's start with healing the feminine and masculine, to bring them back into balance.

Atlantis embodied all the qualities we associate with feminine energy—nurturing, receptive, caring, and supportive. It was a matriarchy but without the emphasis on the female gender, it was more of an energetic concept that embodied predominately the feminine energy. The male qualities of movement, action, and control were not as important. After the fall of Atlantis we decided that having too much of that caring, nurturing energy was not a good thing. So we allowed the male energy—which is more dominant, controlling, directing, and driving—to become the predominant energy within the foundation of the new ascension paradigm. This created a paradigm of control and domination, beginning with the church, which is the concept of man as God, and aligned with humanity's attempt to become greater than God, which is what destroyed Atlantis. In more modern times this control has moved from kings and rulers to corporations and governments.

Overall, this was allowed to happen because we were trying to atone for our role in Atlantis. So we gave power to those who created the destruction in the hope that they would not repeat their actions. By removing the feminine energy, which is shown throughout history as the complete disempowerment of the female, we created an energetic vacuum. What we wanted the male energy to do was realize how they had misused their power, awaken and integrate their feminine side and create the masculine/feminine partnership. This was the lesson of Pangea, in which the Moon, or feminine and love energy, was separated from the Earth. Through the reformation of this union, the control and domination of the male energy could be balanced with the supporting and caring and nurturing of the female energy, for the benefit of both and the detriment of neither.

One of the things we read a lot about in spiritual literature today is the reawakening of the feminine energy. But without the balance of masculine, that will only re-create the problems we experienced in Atlantis where there was so much nurturing that people would not take action, they lost their drive, and could not fully commit to their ascension path.

The gender you have chosen for this lifetime reveals your Atlantean feminine and masculine power issues that you want to heal.

Your choice to experience your lifetime as a woman today enables you to heal lessons in power and control. Much of your life may have been a lesson in learning to overcome many power challenges, beginning with your own mother who, instead of being warm and nurturing may have been controlling and domineering. You may also have had many lessons in powerlessness during the course of your life, from situations in which the only way to overcome them was to find your inner source of power. This is part of your Atlantis Legacy, where you need to learn to balance the nurturing, caring and supportive energies you embody with your feminine energy and not reject the masculine side of your energy, which gives you the power to take action, direct your energy, and learn to user your power to control your life circumstances.

In Atlantis, you fully embodied the feminine nurturing energy and easily shared your power with others. Your fear of integrating the masculine energies lies within your memory of how Atlantis was destroyed, by those who embodied this masculine energy and used it to control others' energy and power. Rather than embracing the energy you remember as being responsible for so much pain, you reject it because you do not want to be part of it. And yet this creates a powerful imbalance that limits your ability to act upon your intentions for yourself and your life.

Integrating the assertive, action-oriented male energies will help you empower your intentions and take action when it is needed. You will no longer feel powerless and will not feel disempowered by those who try to dominate you. And you will no longer attract these dominating energies.

Some women try to work through this by going to extremes. On one side there is the woman who integrates only the feminine energy, rejecting the masculine and who is dominated and powerless in her life. On the other side there is the woman who embraces the masculine, denies the feminine, and becomes a woman who pursues an agenda of domination and control without the nurturing, caring and supportive nature of the feminine.

If you are a male today, one of your Atlantean Paradigm issues is to integrate the feminine energy, which is nurturing, caring and supportive, with the more dominating, controlling male energies. In Atlantis you were either one of the architects of the ascension technology, you participated in its creation, or you watched how this group used its masculine energy to control and dominate the ascension cycle, and eventually destroy Atlantis. You may have guilt or shame over these actions, whether you were a participant or an observer, so you reject the feminine energy, which you see as powerless, weak, and susceptible to being dominated. You may also reject it from the point of your shame at having taken advantage of others' power.

To fulfill the lesson of integrating the feminine energy, some men go completely to the extreme, abandoning their masculinity while trying to embrace the feminine side and they become confused, weak and feel powerless. Other men go to the other extreme, disavowing and rejecting their feminine side to become all masculine and that creates a man who is overly aggressive and detached from his emotions. And both of those aspects are very limiting because on one side there is a man who is caring and nurturing but has no drive, ambition or motivation because he is afraid of what he will do with that power.

And on the other side is the man who has no compassion, emotions or caring for others, who amasses vast amounts of power, often in the form of money, and then uses it to expand his empire and dominate and control others, with no regard for the impact on their lives.

On this healing path you will learn to balance these two aspects within-you so your dominating, action oriented male energy is balanced with the feminine supportive, nurturing energy without being dominated by either and finding new sources and uses of power by being whole and complete within both aspects.

If you think there is a lot of fear ingrained in the overall Atlantean Paradigm and in your Atlantis Legacy, you're right. Where we find this fear is not so much in what we are afraid of, but in where we limit ourselves. Much of the fear came from the final moments of Atlantis, based on your role in the destruction.

Were you a victim, who didn't have any part in the destruction, either as a contributor or a creator of the 'ascension engine' and were part of the collateral damage?

Did you feel betrayed by a trusted friend who convinced you to share your energy and light to help accelerate ascension and destroyed it instead?

Were you one of those who was ridiculed, silenced or rejected because you questioned or were trying to reveal the true motives of the 'ascension engine'?

Did you participate in gathering energy to empower the technology that would accelerate ascension, help develop and build it or promoted it?

Or were you one of the architects of this technology, a creator of the agenda that was supposed to accelerate the ascension cycle and in doing so, were directly responsible for the misuse of Atlanteans' energy and power, and for Atlantis' destruction?

Depending on how you spent your last moments in Atlantis, you created an energetic, fear-based imprint that embodies the guilt, shame, betrayal, remorse, anger, powerlessness, or victimization you felt at that time. This is manifested in your life in many ways, in your soul group, how you limit your life, how you use or do not use your power, how you feel about yourself and in everything you do and do not do. Whatever you fear has its basis in your Atlantean Paradigm fear.

We all share in the Atlantean experience, as it is encoded in our DNA. Especially if you are a teacher, healer, spiritual leader, life coach, author, scientist, computer expert, artist, musician or want to be any of those things, you are expressing, or trying to express, your Atlantean heritage. As you read the list below mark any of the ones that resonate with you because this tells you where you hold your fear.

Being manipulated or taken advantage of by others is at the top of the list because this resonated with most of Atlantis' community, except those who developed the ascension technology. And it is the primary reason why you limit yourself and the expression of your gifts or power, because you do not want to participate in the abuse or misuse of energy in any way.

Accused of not telling the truth or of not being right. There are two different aspects of this fear. The first is being accused of not being right, which is having someone accuse you of manipulating information or of not being truthful, to where you are not telling them the right thing or what you're telling them is wrong. This applies to those who realized they were being lied to by people they trusted, as well as those who were trying to voice their suspicions and were silenced. The second is that you may also doubt what others tell you, doubt their motives and intentions and feel that others don't listen to you or you have a fear of being accused of lying or of your own motives being questioned by others.

Especially if you were one who questioned the process, you express that fear in two ways. First, you want to be beyond reproach. You want to be absolutely one hundred percent right about everything before you share it with others. You may consider yourself a perfectionist but it is more serious than that, you never share any information before you are sure it's correct because you dread experiencing the ramifications of being wrong. And you want to be sure that no one ever questions your integrity or motives. You often spend so much time doubting yourself, your abilities and resources that while it may be your intention to share your gifts, and you never do because you never feel 'perfect' enough.

Another way that you express this, and this is actually two different ways, is you want to make sure that you're always telling the truth. With such a pronounced focus on being truthful, you are surrounded by people who constantly question your integrity or your value. Or you are tirelessly self critical and constantly question your own integrity, truth and value. Either way, you use your quest for perfectionism to become the reason you limit your self expression, embrace your power and share your gifts with others.

Being seen as someone who is powerful and looked up to by others. You may express this by not participating in anything where you can be in a role of leadership or authority. You may avoid any activity or life path in which you must take authority, have others listen to you, or who follow your guidance. Many of those who contributed their power or convinced others to share their power were trusted leaders and were respected and admired by their community.

Having a lot of responsibility to or for others In Atlantis everyone accepted responsibility for the well-being of the community as everything was shared. People trusted each other without question and did what was necessary to take care of themselves and the community. If you feel that you did not perform your responsibility or did something that hurt the community, you would be reluctant to take on that responsibility today. You don't want to be in a situation where you can feel responsible for someone's wellbeing or their future, without regard for the fact that they will make choices about their path and future irrespective of your input. It's interesting that many light workers today who are in their fifties and sixties are being entrusted with the care of children, grandchildren, parents or grandparents, siblings or extended family members because others are not accepting their responsibilities. This is one way that you are healing your Atlantis Legacy with your soul group around this issue.

Others will accuse me of misusing my power. This is one of our primary fears in the context of the Atlantis Legacy and it is easily resolved by not acknowledging your power--if you do not own it or use it, no one can accuse you of misusing. Or you wait to get others' permission to be powerful, usually from other soul group members, so that you feel it is acceptable to them that you express your power and they agree with it. This is another aspect of Atlantean Guilt, having misused power at one time and wanting to ensure that this does not happen again. Power issues are an especially important aspect of the Atlantis Legacy and one we must overcome because it is through accepting, embracing, owning and using our power that we create the energy to empower ascension.

Not using my power in the right and best ways. This fear limits your ability to use your power because you want to ensure that you are not harming, disturbing, upsetting, or challenging anyone when you use your power. Believing you misused your power in Atlantis means that you now you want to ensure that your use of power is impeccable. With this fear you spend a lot of time questioning your motives, and often those of other people, because the right and best use of power is important to you. It is probably hard for you to make final choices because you spend much time doubting yourself and your motivations. And you tend to give a lot of your power away or make a lot of allowances for people in your life because you don't want to be too powerful or more powerful than they are.

My life will be out of my control. This fear encompasses the scenario of the final moments in Atlantis, as people began to realize what was happening and knew that there was nothing they could do to prevent disaster, destruction and death. There was nowhere to go, no way to escape, no higher ground to which they could escape from the water and everyone was in the same situation. No one was in control of what was happening on the

Earth and no one had the ability to stop it. This created the belief that if we begin a process that starts with using our power in some way, the situation will reach a point of no return, where we are unable to stop whatever is happening to us or to those around us.

There is an aspect of this fear in all of the other Atlantis Legacy aspects, the fear that your power will be misused or used, you will be misrepresented or tell people the wrong thing and there will be consequences, you will be accused of not telling the truth when you actually are. It will throw your life into chaos and everything you have done in your life will be completely destroyed. And, once it has begun, you will be powerless to stop the destruction.

Do you see how this is happening today? People are losing their homes, jobs, livelihoods, families are broken up, and it feels like we are not in control of anything any longer. And yet we are losing control of a system which we were never in control of, so we can create a new system that we can control.

Once we find the basis of our fears within our Atlantis Legacy, we find that they are not random and have a very specific beginning in our Atlantis experience. And once we know the fear we can find its solution, through our healing work.

Finding the source of this fear is sometimes as easy as looking at our soul group. You can pinpoint your Atlantean fear source and the type of paradigm you brought into this lifetime through the person who is your biggest challenge, and that can be a parent, sibling, friend, or partner.

What do they do to challenge you?

Do they try to control, manipulate, or dominate you?

Do they keep you in a victim role by being very critical or judgmental or you?

Are they keeping you engaged in some kind of drama or are they very needy?

How do you feel about them?

What do you do to yourself to limit your power with and around them?

Our family of origin, whether that's a birth or adoptive family, is the mirror of our energy, particularly the lower energies of fear, guilt and shame. What you complete the sentence, "In my family I am the one who is..." with says much about your Atlantean fear, your atonement and chosen life path. Are you the different one who is often misunderstood? Are you the victim? Do you feel powerless around this person or those people? Are you the one who is powerful but you limit your power?

When you look at your family as your soul group, without the emotional attachments and expectations you have of the family unit, what you get is a snapshot of your Atlantean energy. How you interact, how they treat you, how you think of them, how they think of you, are all mirrors of the soul imprint that has to do with guilt and shame and atonement and all the fears you have around that, the limitations to using your power, your gifts, etc. Their role in your life is to be your healing teachers, which doesn't include meeting your emotional needs. You have chosen them to help you heal your Atlantis Legacy imprint in this lifetime, so you can complete your ascension journey. While their behavior may hurt and confuse you, it is part of their commitment to you and your healing.

You may also feel responsible for their healing through the guilt and shame you carry with your Atlantean Guilt imprint. The mother who dominated you may be someone whose belief in you ended their life. Your distant father may have been someone you tried to expose as having an agenda of power and control. The people who do not understand you may be those who rejected you in Atlantis and you are trying to get them to see your value now, the value and integrity they could not acknowledge in you then. What we do not consider is those who victimize, criticize, judge and control us are also operating from their own guilt and shame imprints that are part of their Atlantis Legacy. As you consider the challenging person or people in your life, consider whether their actions or behavior are prompted by the guilt or shame they feel for what they have done to you as part of your shared Atlantis experience.

As we move forward through this section on healing, pay attention to the people who come to mind as we are completing these exercises because they are the ones you will release and in doing so, you also release them from holding this healing space for you.

Reclaiming Your Atlantis Gifts

Everyone had a role in Atlantis, according to their gifts, talents and abilities. This was their work, how their needs were met and how they contributed to the overall community. Since everyone did work that was related to their gifts and talents, their work was simply part of their life. A musician was someone who had musical talent they shared with others. A teacher was one who had wisdom to share. Someone who had an interest in science became a scientist. A gardener was someone who had a talent for growing beautiful plants. There was no concept of working for others in jobs they did not like, being unsure of their gifts or talents or wondering how they were going to make a living and taking a job because it was available or it was all they were offered, as we do today.

We carried these roles and interests into our lives today except, with the Atlantis Legacy, we can limit our ability or willingness to express our gifts. There is a great deal of information about your legacy from what you do not think you can do, do not allow yourself to do, or prevent yourself from doing. This is a sure sign that whatever you are resisting is part of your Atlantean experience.

As you read through the following list, and it includes some of the more general roles that can actually be expanded to include many different types of activities, mark which one(s) resonate with you or appeal to you. You may not be doing those things in your line of work today but this may give you insight into what you can do with your life to use your gifts, and the kinds of gifts and talents you have, even if they are hidden from your awareness.

I like creating things and am very artistic or musical. I am a musician or artist or I enjoy crafts-related hobbies

I enjoy writing and sharing information with others through writing or speaking. I am an author and/or speaker, I have a training background or have always been pulled in that career direction.

I enjoy research and learning about new things. I am very curious and always want to know more about things. I have always had a strong interest in science or in finding out more about the Earth, the universe, and am intrigued by all aspects of science.

I enjoy building things, working with my hands and work on projects or hobbies. I am an architect, builder, do home remodeling, would like that as a career or part-time job.

I enjoy cooking, food, gardening, and being in nature. I am happiest when I am working with the Earth, water, and doing things that help or nurture the Earth. I would enjoy being a gardener or chef, naturalist, botanist, or being near the ocean, mountains or in the country.

I am passionate about helping others, especially those who cannot help themselves. I am a lawyer or people have said I would make a good lawyer, judge or advocate.

I feel the need to be in control of my life and environment and will do what I can to ensure that I am always in control. If I am part of a group, I am the one who is chosen as leader.

There are people who have no desire to be a leader but who are very creative and very musical. Or there are people who cringe at the thought of writing something but are very good at building or creating—being an architect, builder, seamstress, gardener, landscape artist, interested in wood working, or someone who likes to fix up old furniture, would be something that they either do today or that they are interested in. They like to create things, to build things, to see new things take shape. What appeals to you the most is the area in which your gifts lie. If you are passionate about writing, that is your gift. If you are scared to death of writing, even though it's something you really like to do and may even do in secret without showing anyone your work that is a limitation imposed by your Atlantis Legacy.

How does that work? Fear, guilt and shame create limitations. For example, when you consider today that you would like to have a joyful, happy, abundant life in which you do work you love and you feel very successful, do you feel guilty about being happy?

Do you feel that you don't deserve it or you shouldn't have it?

Do you feel that it will be taken away from you or be a source of pain or problems?

Or do you feel that if you create this wonderful life and you're really happy that you're not going to be fulfilling your healing mission with your soul group?

And that last statement is the most important because within that context are the needs of your soul group and how you address them through the lens of your Atlantean Guilt. To fulfill your mission of atonement you believe that you need to take care of others before you take care of yourself even though you may be guided to do other things. Or you're going to be the source of others' pain because you will be someone they look up to and you may disappoint them, or you will be accused, rejected, denied, persecuted or threatened by others because you are successful.

How do you limit your growth and expansion? Three possible ways are that you don't believe in yourself, you don't trust your abilities, or you are afraid of your power. Others may pertain to your individual situation, so pay attention to what comes to mind when you think about this subject.

As I was writing the material for the class on which this book is based, a topic that came up as another strong source of limitation is what we fear the most as a life experience. The one that arose for me is a fear of drowning in the ocean. Although I love the ocean, my love for it is accompanied by a healthy respect for its dangers. I will go in the water up to my knees, maybe a little bit higher, and that's about it. I cannot go into water that's above my head in the ocean, although I'm a very good swimmer. My Atlantis life ended by drowning, as did that of many others there. But I learned, while preparing the material for this book, that I drowned because I was locked in a prison cell and could not escape. I was locked away because I was trying to expose the true agenda of the ascension technology. The person who imprisoned me, a member of my soul group and part of my birth family today, did not come to rescue me.

As a result, I am claustrophobic today and wherever I am, I always need to know where the exit is located. As a child, I would have nightmares about being locked in a room and not being able to find the door to get out. During these nightmares I would sleepwalk around the house, searching for the door, crying because I could not find it. In this lifetime, while I have never been to jail, I also avoid any activities that would put me there. It has been very hard for me to accept my role as a teacher and spiritual guide and share my work in a public way.

While Atlantis did not originally have the concept of jails or prison, some of you who were questioning the agenda of the ascension acceleration plan were locked away or isolated. And many of you died in these places as the water covered the Earth. So if you have a fear of going to jail, or have been in jail, if you are claustrophobic of have a fear of speaking or sharing your information, these all have Atlantean origins. You may also have a fear of starvation or homelessness, of water, cold, or of drowning. Some of you may have never learned how to swim because you are afraid of the water.

Knowing your fears around these life experiences is powerful insight into what may have happened to you during your final days or moments in Atlantis.

If you didn't feel restricted in using your power, what would you be doing now? If you felt completely free to use your power in any way you wanted to, what would you be doing? When I asked this question of myself the answer surprised me. I have always been musically talented and can play several musical instruments. The answer I got was that I would not have married or had children when I did, I would have become a drummer in a rock and roll band. It's something I had briefly considered as a teenager but never pursued.

Now I feel I could do that. And to confirm this as the truth for me, a few weeks after I had this realization, Kenny Aronoff, one of the world's best rock and roll drummers, who has played with some of the world's top bands, and David Santos, a bassist for the band Santana, both sat next to me on an airplane and we talked for several hours. They both told me that the industry didn't have enough women drummers, age wasn't important, and if that was my dream, I should pursue it and they would support me. Wow, what a gift and confirmation!

Does this question begin to open some doors of potential for you? The limitations that exist in your life are imposed by your Atlantis Legacy fears and obligations, and you live your life through them.

If they were not there, what would you be doing with your life right now? The answer to this question allows you to open yourself up to expressing your gifts without guilt or shame Pay attention to your answer to this question because it will be used in some of the healing work we do later.

Once you give yourself permission to explore your potential, outside of your Atlantean Paradigm and its obligations, you can learn much about the gifts and talents you have hidden from yourself. When you ask yourself certain questions you open your heart to receiving the answers. Questions such as:

I know that I can -- This is pointing you in the direction of your strengths and your abilities. What do you know that you excel at, in spite of your fears and doubts? It might be writing, singing, painting, cooking a nutritious meal, playing the piano, being a good listener. Don't judge your answers by whether or not you think they are important.

I have always wanted to -- Maybe you always wanted to be a ballerina or to sing, write, travel or visit Egypt or to go to Africa. There's something that you've always wanted to do that maybe you've never shared with anyone but it's a desire you have had for a long time. Be bold, courageous and creative with this answer.

I wish that I could -- Is there something you wish you could do? Wishes are the voice of your heart speaking to you. So when you say, "Oh, I wish that I could write a book" or whatever it is you wish that you could do, that's your heart opening you to a new potential for your gifts and your life.

I don't think that I am worthy of -- This is where you limit ability to express and manifest the answers to the first three questions. Do you think you are worthy of joy, love, abundance, success, fulfillment, peace, or of doing things you enjoy? We also hear this question when we think we are not worthy of fulfilling our heart's desire. When you answer this question you may hear the voice of someone telling you that you were not good enough, couldn't do something or they didn't believe in you. And that's an important voice to listen to because that is also the echo of your own Atlantean Paradigm energy.

I am afraid that -- What are you afraid might happen if you pursue your dreams? Whatever you're afraid of is a manifestation of your Atlantis Legacy. And it also reveals your Atlantean Guilt with a deep fear of potential repercussions that arise if you do not honor your commitments to heal, atone, and meet the needs of your soul group. This causes you to consider you life choices in the context of the level of responsibility you feel for others' lives, which includes how they live their life and the results they achieve. Many insights about your limitations can be revealed when you know what you are afraid of and why.

Release Soul Group Commitments

You have made strong commitments to your soul group and hold yourself accountable for their healing. These are powerful soul contracts which have a profound connection to our Atlantean Paradigm and Atlantean Guilt. Karmic cycles are behind these contracts and they have strong emotional energy that binds us together until one of us releases the commitment. These are commitments for healing and atonement that you made in a moment of fear and they work in many ways. For example, you can be connected to those whose lives you feel responsible for and that ended because of your involvement in Atlantis' destruction. Whether you tried to warn them and they didn't listen, or you innocently promoted the technology, you were an innocent victim, or you saw their death, the feelings of guilt, responsibility and atonement are the same. Through this connection you may martyr or victimize yourself, or allow them to be needy and draw on your energy.

Or you and your soul group can hold each other hostage energetically, demanding an exchange of energy and power because of your shared experiences in Atlantis. This could involve taking care of a sick parent you are estranged from or who has been abusive, unkind, distant or uncaring, or providing a family member with financial support that you cannot afford. You can also be martyring yourself in the hope that you receive acknowledgement, support, and validation from those you rejected you or whom you tried to warn of the impending Atlantean disaster. Here you could limit your choice of profession because you know they would not approve or support your choice.

These powerful commitments control how you live your life but they are commitments that you have taken under strong, self-imposed emotional pressure. And there is a great deal of fear around them and what happens to you and your soul group members if do not honor them.

What are you afraid will happen if you do not honor your commitments to your soul group? If you do not follow through, what do you think will happen to you? Or to them?

The truth that we do not realize is that nothing will happen to either one of us. We can release these commitments any time we want to and there will be no ramifications, no judgment and no repercussions. But until we know that, we will continue to stay in the karmic cycles of our soul commitments, limiting our lives because of the responsibility we have committed ourselves to through our Atlantis-based guilt and shame.

Our soul group members, through their own Atlantis Legacy, may be looking for someone to blame for what happened to them and they will use your guilt to extract their revenge. In this way you become the object of their anger even though you may not have been responsible for any of it. What we do not consider within soul group contracts, karmic cycles and commitments is that everyone is responsible for their reality, both the victim and the aggressor. Each person shares some aspect of responsibility for what happened and all must acknowledge their power by claiming ownership of the part they are responsible for. For example, the person who feels victimized by their Atlantean experience will carry that victim energy throughout their lifetimes, being victimized by people and life circumstances in each one, until they accept responsibility for the part they played in creating that situation.

Think of a person in your life you feel you have a soul commitment with, someone whose life you feel responsible for.

What happens if you release yourself from this commitment?

What are you afraid will happen to them?

In what way are you responsible for that?

Can you release yourself from this commitment and let them find their own healing path?

Do you know what your soul group commitments are?

Have you ever explored this topic? Your soul group commitments are what you have committed your time and energy to do on behalf of your soul group. You can start to unveil them by writing this statement on a piece of paper: "I have committed to help my soul group to…" and then writing down whatever information you receive. The results may surprise you. You may have committed to helping them heal, to avoid pain, to be successful, realize their power, to help them overcome their limitations, to provide emotional or financial support.

These are all very noble commitments. However, one of the ways that you honor them is by sharing your own power with them, limiting the options in your life whose potential fulfillment conflicts with your soul group commitments. While the first part of the soul commitment promise is that you will help them do something, the second part states how you will limit your life to do it, or what you will give up in your life to ensure they have it in theirs. You help them as opposed to expanding your own energy and letting them learn by observing your joy, success, and abundance. That's one of the things we're going to clear as we do our clearing exercises in the next section, the limitations you created in your commitment to heal your soul group. It is time to realize that they bear some of the responsibility for allowing themselves to be swept away, literally and figuratively, in Atlantis.

As much as you show others your commitment to them by being present for them, by suffering for them, by suffering with them, by being beside them on their journey, they don't understand or appreciate the sacrifice you're making. They also don't do any healing because they don't have anything to heal into. You have become the light, energy and power in their lives. So there is nothing for them to do, other than to continue to draw power, energy and light from you, simply because it's available. And you get caught up in their victim cycle and become a victim with them.

As you write down some of the things that you have committed to helping your soul group do in their lives, you can also look at how you have set up your life to allow them to do that.

Do you limit your power because you know that they are afraid of it? And if you are in your power they will distance themselves from you? Do you limit your success because you know they will not be able to achieve that level of success in their own lives?

Do you limit your joy because you know that they are unhappy?

Do you limit love in your life because they don't have love in theirs?

Now consider this, if you were not doing these things in your life, if you end your soul contracts and commitments, if you live the life you want to live and make choices for yourself, what kind of life would you have?

Are you willing to do that?

If so, the next section will help you release your soul contracts and commitments, to release your Atlantis Legacy, your part of the Atlantean Paradigm, and Atlantean Guilt so you can create a new paradigm for your life and invite higher frequencies into your life to move forward on your ascension journey.

In this section you will find clearing exercises that can help you release your Atlantis Legacy, the Atlantean Guilt and Atlantean Paradigm. You will also replace what you release with greater intention for yourself, your life and the use of your power and gifts.

Embracing Your Atlantis Role

The first clearing exercise is to help you remember your Atlantean role, which is the work you did in Atlantis. So often, this is the path we want to take today but deliberately reject it, even though it is the one which will bring us the most fulfillment. To refresh your memory, here is the list of the types of roles that were known in Atlantis. This is a very general list so choose the type of role that you feel resonates the most with you or write your own, even if it is not something you do right now.

If you already wrote down which ones you resonate with from an earlier chapter, you may use that list.

I like creating things and am very artistic or musical. I am a musician or artist or I enjoy hobbies, crafts, anything that allows me to create something.

I enjoy writing and sharing information with others through writing or speaking. I am an author and/or speaker, I have a training background or have always been pulled in that career direction.

I enjoy research and learning about new things. I am very curious and always want to know more about things. I have always had a strong interest in science or in finding out more about the Earth, the universe, and am intrigued by all aspects of science.

I enjoy building things, working with my hands and work on projects or hobbies. I am an architect, builder, do home remodeling, would like that as a career or part-time job.

I enjoy cooking, food, gardening, and the Earth. I am happiest when I am working with the earth and growing things. I would enjoy being a gardener or chef, living by the ocean or in the mountains. I am happiest when I am in nature, I love animals and I love the Earth..

I am passionate about helping others, especially those who cannot help themselves. I am a lawyer or people have said I would make a good lawyer, judge or advocate.

I feel the need to be in control of my life and environment and will do what I can to ensure that I am always in control. If I am part of a group, I am the one who is chosen as leader.

When you get to the role that resonates the most with you, and you should read all of them, breathe in the joy of doing that role.

If you are the role of the creator and you enjoy making and creating things, one of your roles is to bring beauty to the world, to show people new ways of communication through the powerful creative language of their heart using art, music, and many other types of creativity that enhances their lives. This is your gift to share with the world. Breathe out and release any fear of not being appreciated, any resentment or doubt about your abilities. Breathe out and release any limitation you have to the expression of that role within you because you don't want it to be interpreted improperly, you don't want people to misunderstand, you don't want it to be used against you or taken away from you. You have a gift that helps people see the world in a more expanded and expansive way. Accept your role as a creator, as a musician, as an artist, as someone who shares that gift with the world so that you can inspire others to see the world in this way for themselves.

If you are a writer and you enjoy sharing information and communicating with people, your gift is not only to reach out to them from your own heart space, but also how to listen to their own hearts because through sharing what you know you opens them up to voices within themselves that they haven't been able to hear yet. Focus on the joy that people have when they read your writing, and their lives are enhanced from what you share. Breathe out and release any fear you have of sharing your messages with the world, of not being perfect, of misleading others, of being judged or criticized. This is how you make peace with your role as you learn to view it as the blessing it once was for you.

Breathe out any limitations you have to sharing the truth in your heart, to communicating your ideas and your thoughts to others for fear that they'll be misinterpreted, misused, not accepted or judged. Or the fear that you will lead them astray because everyone is responsible for their understanding and for their actions.

And then accept yourself as a conveyer of information and as someone through whom divine messages flow in ways that encompass your energy and the teachings that you have for the world. Know that the right audience for you is the one that will be able to hear you and to resonate with you and to see the truth of what you say. Also as part of this particular role, release any fear of being misinterpreted, misquoted or your words misused and know that all you are responsible for is sharing the words that you hear—nothing else.

If you enjoy building, creating and making things you are a creator, someone who creates things that other people can enjoy, that enhances their life in some way. This is your gift. And the fear that this gift will be misused, that you'll create structures that people will not use to the right advantage, or not use in the right way is something that you have allowed to limit the expression of this gift in your life.

111

Breathe out any resistance to using your gifts in this way, any resentment towards others who have misused your gift at any point in time—those who have been jealous of you, those who have insinuated their way into your work or even those who have taken your work and used it for themselves or used it in some way to hurt you or others. And then acknowledge yourself as a creator, as a builder, as someone who enjoys creating beautiful things, whether they're physical structures or spiritual structures that other people can find joy and pleasure in.

Those of you who are advocates for others and who have the gift of being able to help other people, one of the things to release is your need to help others because you feel they can't help themselves and to feel responsible for doing things for people that you think they are incapable of doing. It makes you feel very powerless and helpless in the face of so much need.

One of the things to release at this time is your desire to right any wrongs you think you have committed. Shift that to a desire to reveal what is right and to help people see the rightness and the truth of themselves and of every situation so that you can help them create their own truth and become their own advocates. Release any responsibility for others' destruction or results and instead, take responsibility for ensuring that they have the right information to find their own transformation and to create their own ascension. Everything that you are speaking the truth about, everything you advocate for stops at the point where you deliver the information. You cannot take responsibility for what people do with it.

If you have very strong leadership energies you are concerned that you will always lead people in the right direction. And one of the ways you prevent this from happening is by not acknowledging yourself as a leader. Release the guilt over having led people in the wrong direction, or having been unable to prevent situations from happening, or have had your power misused or have even had your words misinterpreted or misconstrued or your power usurped by someone. One of the things that you need to understand about this role is that you have come into this new ascension paradigm as a leader—whether you are actually physically leading people or you are in that position of managing or controlling or directing or sharing information that inspires others to lead, whether that's leading themselves or leading others. The fear of this being somehow misconstrued or mismanaged or misinterpreted is very strong within you and it prevents you from truly acknowledging yourself as a leader and from allowing yourself to express that leadership in yourself but also to inspire others to be leaders.

Release the fear that you're going to be taken advantage of or that you will lead people astray or that through your leadership abilities people will believe and trust you, and through circumstances outside of your control you will lead them to their destruction. This role has the most guilt associated with it because as a leader, you felt responsible for the guidance you shared and for having led others astray, consciously or unconsciously. As a leader you are to inspire others to rise to their power, and to accept their own leadership roles. You do that by encouraging them to go within and to be inspired in spirit within themselves, which is one of the roles you play in the new earth today.

Clearing your Soul Group Legacy

You were asked to write down the name of the soul group that you feel most challenged by and this could be anybody in your life, a parent, sister or brother or other family member. It also could be a child, friend, spouse, partner, neighbor, co-worker, spouse, partner or ex-partner. Think of the one person you feel most challenged by right now. You can do this exercise as many times as you want, with as any different people as you need to. In this moment, think of the person you feel most responsible for, who has been your greatest source of commitment, as well the strongest symbol of your Atlantean guilt and/or shame.

First we are going to clear your guilt over your role in whatever happened to them and in order to do that I'd like for you to see them standing in front of you. And this can be done with anyone, living or dead. It is effective with anyone because we are working from the level of energy and spirit.

Imagine that challenging person standing in front of you. Ask your Higher Self to be present with you as you do this clearing work and you can see your Higher Self standing next to you, or next to the person you are working with.

Now ask your Higher Self to reveal your feelings, emotions, and beliefs around this person from the Atlantean timeline.

You may feel very guilty and almost unable to face them because you're seeing them from both your Atlantis experience and how you relate today. Whether you realize it or not, as soon as they appear before you, you step back into your Atlantean role and you may suddenly feel strong emotions such as guilt or anger. You may feel ashamed. This emotional response happens because when you connect with them at any time, because they are part of your soul group, you have an energetic imprint that is activated with them. While you may consider them as part of your life in the current lifetime, you are always energetically connected to them through the paradigm of your Atlantis lifetime and that's why they are such a challenge to you now.

The first thing to do is to release the energy of atonement. You can do this by forgiving them for not listening to you or heeding your wisdom or advice. Look at them, looking into their eyes if you can, and say simply, "I forgive you for not listening to me, for not hearing me, for not taking my advice and for not valuing my advice or information. I now release you into the lessons of the responsibility you hold as creator of your reality."

The guilt that you feel is over your lack of control in the situation, which you could not control although you feel that you should have. You have accepted responsibility for something they had an equal or greater responsibility to control and they did not. When you forgive them, you forgive them for not using their power, for doing things that created their own destruction and you give back the responsibility for their life to them.

Imagine something in your hands that represents their responsibility and give it to them and say,

"You are responsible for your life and for your death. And I return the responsibility for this back to you. We are both free from the emotional connections that this has created between us."

And then if you see any cords that lead from them to you—you may have been aware of them before or you may be aware of them now—just disconnect those cords from you and from them, wherever they are connected. You do the disconnection because you are releasing both yourself and them, and this completes the release of the energy between you.

Healing the Energy Connection

Now you will heal the point of energetic connection with this person. To do this you will first discover the point of connection and then use the light from the crystalline matrix above your head, which you pull into your body through your crown chakra, and use the light to heal this point of connection.

First, ask your Higher Self to show you that point within you where the connection to this person exists.

It may be in the root chakra, around your tail bone at the base of your spine. This is also where we hold tribal, community, or family energy.

It may be in the second chakra, around your pelvic bone, which manages sexual energy, gender issues, and male/female energy.

Or it may be in your solar plexus located in the center of your rib cage, near your navel. This is where we hold power issue.

It may be in your heart chakra, at the center of your chest near your sternum. Our emotional issues, including heartbreak and guilt, are held here.

Or it may be in your throat chakra, at the base of your throat, which has to do with speech, speaking, losing your voice or not using your voice.

It may be in your third eye in the center of your forehead, which is also where we hold our ability to 'see' the through the veil between the material and spiritual worlds.

Or your crown chakra, at the top of your head, which is your connection to the divine energy of Source. We hold issues of separation and disconnection from Source here.

Find a place within you where you feel that you are disempowered by this person or experience you share with them. This could also be where you disempower yourself.

Bring in light from the crystalline matrix above your head, draw it into your crown chakra at the top of your head and down to the chakra that you have recognized as a source of disempowerment.

As you send light to this area, set an intention to heal the disempowerment, remove the connection and raise its vibration to the highest possible level.

Connecting with the Full Expression of Your Power

Once you have done that, you will also use the light to expand your physical body to accept the fullness of your power. Tell your Higher Self you want to create a connection to the full scope of your power.

Now pull in more light from the crystalline matrix above your head and imagine that with this light, you are also receiving the gift of your power pouring into your body. Be open to receiving the full expression of your power.

Allow your physical body to expand and make yourself bigger, to where you are eight feel tall, then ten, then as big as your house. Expand your body as you are receiving the full expression of your power so you can have a visual image of how much power you have.

You may be surprised at how big you are becoming. Continue to draw in light and make yourself as big as you need to be. You can expand your size to as big as the earth, the Sun, to the edge of the universe.

Your physical size becomes a manifestation of the fullness of your power that you will allow yourself to expand into.

Your body, your spirit will let you know how big you need to get to feel fully within your power and energy. Continue to expand until you feel that where you are is the full expression of your power. Celebrate your size and take a moment to appreciate what this power feels like.

Reveal your Power Expression to your Soul Group

Look down at the person you have been working with, who has been your greatest challenging and is now standing in front of you. You may find that you dwarf them, that they are tiny little pinpricks and you're miles above them. You may feel a profound sense of joy and deep healing as your soul has been waiting for this moment where it can get out of the little box you have put it in and expand to its full size. And for some of you this may be a surprise because you're finding that you're expanding to be much greater than you thought you were.

From the place of your expanded self, invite the person you have been working with into that space. Invite them to stand next to you and experience the fullness of your power and energy and to know that they too can experience the full power and energy of who they are. And in the fullness now of who you are forgive yourself for your role that you played—whatever role you think that is—in their death and in the death of others in your soul group and anyone else whose death you feel you are responsible for. Just forgive yourself. No explanations, no long winded requirements—just repeat "I forgive myself." And feel what it feels like to be that expanded self that you probably have not experienced since Atlantis.

And now from this point of your expanded self—because you're still this very, very big and tall person—invite the rest of your soul group to join you in this space so they can also experience you in the full expansion of your energy. You do not have to name your soul group members, if you issue the invitation to your soul group from Atlantis to join you, they will be there.

As you extend the invitation, say "I invite my soul group from Atlantis to appear before me," and give them a few seconds to appear. You may be surprised at who appears or the number of people, as this will be a large group. You will see family, friends, siblings, partners, and people you didn't think were part of your Atlantis experience. Let them enter this space and find their place next to you or in front of you.

When they have all gathered, repeat this statement, "I now release all energy of atonement for any Atlantean Guilt or shame that I carry towards you and I release you from all soul group connections with me." You can repeat it once more for emphasis, "I now release all energy of atonement for any Atlantean Guilt or shame that I carry towards you and I release you from all soul group connections with me."

If you see any cords connected to any of them you can release them now, wherever they are connected to them or to you. Some of them may be connected to your heart chakra or your solar plexus. Some of them may be connected to your lower chakra, especially the root chakra.

Release Your Soul Group From Your Shared Legacy

And one more thing that you can do with your soul group still standing in front of you, is to release them from their Atlantis Legacy energies that they have used to connect with you. You may see a very large cord that is connected to you and to the soul group. Release that cord now by using your intention to disconnect it or you can reach down with your hand and physically disconnect it. As you are releasing it, let go of all of the Atlantean connections you have with this soul group.

Release all fears, all blocks, all limitations, any anger, all guilt and shame now.

And you are also releasing them from your obligation to help them change their Atlantean paradigm, to help them atone for anything that they did or didn't do, any powerlessness, any unwillingness to listen, any fear over that particular situation. You're releasing them from that paradigm and all of its associated energies with you.

Expand Yourself to Match Your Energy

And now standing within the full expansion of your energy, which may be a little difficult to hold as you are holding a great deal of energy that you have not held before. You may have never allowed yourself to experience the full expansiveness of who you are, expanding your physical self large enough to hold all of your energy. And it's an exercise that I suggest that you do occasionally, at least once a week, to remind yourself of how expansive your power is and how expansive your energy is.

As you are in this fully expanded version of yourself, ask that the gifts that you have denied, that you have relinquished, and that you have set aside, because of your fear and guilt, enter your energetic space now. Ask your Higher Self to help you release anything that blocks their integration.

You are making room in your energetic space for the gifts that you have abandoned, all the ones that you have denied yourself, that you have thought you weren't good at or refused to look at. Put out a blank call for their return and see what comes in for you. Don't try to name them or to predict what comes up; simply invite anything that is part of your gifts to join you in your energetic space.

Pause for a moment and see what gifts reveal themselves to you.

You may be surprised that you have a new level of creativity, you have a new talent or a hidden talent that suddenly bursts forth. You may have an idea for something you want to write or something you want to create.

And now to keep all the energy kind of contained that you've just created within yourself, before you shrink yourself back down to your normal size I want you to focus on your heart chakra, located just below your sternum or breastbone. Send out a beam of light from your heart chakra and create a big cocoon of light that completely enfolds you. Make sure that it goes all the way around you, from over the top of your head to under your feet, all the way around you, front to back. This will prevent you from leaking more energy out into your Atlantis Legacy and paradigm until it is fully healed. It also prevents you from losing the connection to your gifts as their presence is still new and unfamiliar. New energy paradigms take some time to integrate as our energy has to shift to accommodate them. The cocoon of light will help keep your energy levels intact until you are ready to embrace the new energy levels and align with the energy of your gifts

Set a New Intention for your Life

Continue to send out light and empower your cocoon of light and from within this cocoon of light—and you are still your expanded self—set an intention for your life, for the creation of your new ascension energy. You will no longer be focused on avoiding the outcomes of Atlantis, but for creating a new intention for the new Earth that you are creating with your life.

This is a personal intention for the joy, abundance, success, happiness, and love. Anything you want in your life, set an intention for that. It could be to have a million dollars. It could be to move to Rome. Do not judge what you ask for and do not worry about creating anything too outrageous, everything is a potential for your life.

Once you are free of the Atlantean paradigm you can set an intention for your own heaven on Earth and this is bringing back the very best of the Atlantean energies to your current reality. So all the joy, all the nurturing, support and caring, all the abilities, all of the wonderful things that you could do, the amazing gifts you had, bring that energy back into your new energetic paradigm.

You can do that once you are free of the guilt and shame, and of the Atlantis soul group connections you embodied and that have prevented you from manifesting them. Breathe your new intention deeply into your heart and as you breathe out, expand your intention so that every cell of your body is empowered with your new intention.

Take in another breath and as you breathe out, focus on your root chakra, at the base of your spine, empowering it with your new intention for your life.

Now take your focus to your second chakra, around your pelvis and empower it with your new intention for your life.

Move your focus up to your third chakra, around your navel, and empower it with your new intention for your life.

Bring your intention up to your heart chakra, around your sternum, and empower it with your new intention for your life.

Bring your intention up to your throat chakra, at the base of your neck, and empower it with your new intention for your life.

Bring your intention up to your third eye, in the middle of your forehead, and empower it with your new intention for your life.

And move your intention up to your crown chakra, at the top of your head, and empower it with your new intention for your life.

And now with your new intention for your life firmly around you and firmly grounded within you, one final thing to do with the Atlantean energies is the forgiveness and the release of all the Atlantean energies.

Forgive and Release All Atlantis Energy

As you are standing in your most expanded self with your new intention for your life that incorporates the most wonderful aspects of all of your ascension past, of all of your ascension cycle history with all of the ascension cycles you have experienced, forgiveness, healing and transformation have been the deepest desire of your soul throughout all of your lifetimes. What is it you have always wanted to do, to become, to have in your life? This is your heart's deepest desire and you've carried this with you many, many lifetimes. It is now time to give life to it by removing every block to its manifestation that you have ever created.

You can now allow that to happen by forgiving and releasing all Atlantean energies that you carry. Begin forgiving yourself for everything that was done, that was said, that was not said, everything that was done to you, or in spite of you. Release the memories of the destruction, the grief of seeing everything wiped away, the powerlessness you felt knowing that once this process had started it could not be stopped, the fear of the retribution from God, which has been part of our disconnection is the fear over having let God down, let Source down, or betrayed Source, and betrayed our power.

Forgive yourself for the many, many lives that were lost, the many dreams that were erased, the many people who suffered, for your inability, whether it was conscious or unconscious, to prevent this from happening.

If you were one of those who willingly gave your power for what you thought was a greater good forgive yourself for that, for trusting, for giving your power away, for the responsibility that you shared, for promoting this as an option to those who knew you and loved you and looked up to you.

Forgive yourself for misleading others, consciously or unconsciously, along what you thought was the right path and instead leading them to their destruction.

Forgive yourself for having been weak, for not having spoken up when you knew you should have, for not having been listened to when you thought you could have been more forceful, more direct, more vocal in expressing the truth. And forgive yourself for hurting the Earth and causing destruction to the Earth.

Forgive those who hurt, betrayed, rejected, silenced or opposed you.

Forgive yourself for the pain you caused in the galactic community, for their hopes and dreams of ascension that were lost through the destruction of Atlantis.

And now take your awareness through the top of your head, through your crown chakra to the crystalline matrix above your head, to beyond the crystalline matrix, past the central Sun , see an opening into the universe opening beyond that and move your awareness into the brilliant white light that you imagine as being Source or God.

The Source Forgiveness Exercise

And if you feel you need it, because it is not necessary, ask God to forgive you and acknowledge to God that you forgive yourself. And then from that Source light above your head imagine a beam of unconditional love in the form of a brilliant white light that comes down through that opening, all the way down into your crown chakra.

As you pull the light in through your crown chakra start sending that light all the way through your body, from the top of your head, past your face, into your neck, into your arms, down through your torso, through your hips, into your legs.

And as it's going through your body, keep pushing the light through your body, imagine that it is pulling every shred of memory, every bit of anger, of guilt and shame, all fear, regret, and blame, every association to Atlantis that is connected to you, out of your body.

Let the light collect any energy associated with your Atlantean Paradigm, Legacy and Atlantean Guilt, and if you feel resistance in any area, stay with that area a moment and send more light to it.

Allow the light take all of that energy out of you, then push it out of the soles of your feet and into the ground beneath you.

Now breathe in another beam of light from Source and set an intention for it to heal every bit of anger, of guilt and shame, all fear, regret, and blame, every association to Atlantis that is connected to you, that you have held in your body, on all levels of physical, emotional, and spiritual DNA, all cellular memory, all of the energetic frequencies and vibrations you have held, ask the light to heal all of this in you.

You can do this several times if you need to, pull in light from the Source light above your head and push it through your body, asking it to remove all connections to the Atlantean Paradigm and Atlantean Guilt and release it to the ground through the soles of your feet.

Then pull in light for healing and set an intention for it to heal all of these aspects and energies within you.

Take in as much light as you need to do, pulling in the light as you breathe in and pushing the light down through your body as you breathe out, until you feel this cleansing process is complete.

You can repeat this exercise as many times as you need to by pulling in the light from Source through your crown chakra, allow it to pick up any emotional and energetic residue from your Atlantean experience. And then push it out through your feet into the Earth. Once that is complete, allow yourself to embrace your new intention for your life.

Connecting with the 5th Dimension

And now one last thing we're going to do to complete the healing exercises is bring in the energy of the fifth dimension. Once you've released your Atlantean paradigm you are ready to step into a fifth dimensional or higher experience of life. It doesn't mean you leave the third dimension or your body. It just means that you leave behind a lot of things that have kept you grounded in the energy of the third dimension because of your guilt, shame, and your soul group obligations and commitments. Once you are willing to step out of that energy cycle and you clear it, you can replace it with a higher level of energetic experience.

This is ascension, plain and simple. It does not require fanfare, a big ceremony, special rituals or extravagant details. It is an act of surrender, in which we stop fighting the process and an act of will, in which we use our free will to 'willingly' choose it.

We connect to the fifth dimension from the high heart chakra, which is the higher frequency of the heart chakra. It is located above the heart chakra, midway between the base of the throat and the sternum or heart chakra. You can tap this area lightly and it will probably be sore, that is because we carry our deepest wounds in this area.

Now focus your vision on a spot about three feet directly in front of you. This is the location of the veil that separates the material and spiritual worlds. As you focus on the veil, notice a light that begins to shine behind it and see that light growing bigger and brighter.

Keep your focus on the light in front of you, breathe in and begin to open your high heart chakra as widely as you can. It will open like the petals of a flower, with an outward motion. Breathe out and let your high heart chakra complete its opening until you feel that it is fully open.

Ask the veil in front of you to open, take in a breath and bring the light from the veil towards you, into your open high heat chakra. Continue to breathe in and out, relax, and let the light fill your high heart chakra. You will take in all of the light that you need to. This is a light source you always have access to, which contains the higher vibrations and frequencies, the connection to the knowledge that you have that allows you to incorporate fifth dimensional living into a third dimensional body.

Continue to breathe in and out and take in as much light as you need. When you have taken enough light into your heart chakra, breathe out, pause and see how you feel. You should feel lighter and brighter, you may feel a little lightheaded or emotional. This connection is always available to you so you do not have to overdose on it now. It can make you a little lightheaded or nauseous if you take in too much. As you learn to work with it, you will be able to take in greater amounts and integrate it into your own energetic system. You may want to start with small doses at first as you learn how to balance and integrate this energy within yourself.

Fifth dimensional energy displaces a lot of emotional energy so the emotional energy can rise to the surface with this exercise and may be expressed through tears or laughter or crying or joy. You may feel like crying and laughing at the same time and that's OK. As we practice with it, we will learn to integrate this energy.

You can also use this exercise to set an intention to activate higher dimensions of frequency, beyond the fifth dimension. A word of caution here, you cannot integrate energy that you cannot align with or integrate and it's a process. So if you are energetically prepared for the fifth dimension, it will not be more beneficial to try to access the seventh, for example. First, you won't be able to access that dimensional level because you are not aligned with it, and second, if you did it would not be very helpful or feel very good because you cannot take in more energy than your body is physically able to align with.

Use this exercise at least once a day, it only takes a few minutes, as it takes time for your body to integrate and align with higher dimensional frequencies. It does displace lower level emotional energies so you may feel very emotional, cry, or feel different as you work with this energy.

By using it daily you help your body integrate the energy more smoothly and in a balanced way. There is no harm in 'forgetting', that is your body's way of telling you that it has enough and needs time to integrate before you take on any more. You can't take it all in at once and be done with it. Faster is not better, this was one of the lessons of Atlantis. This is an exercise in balance and integration so you have to give yourself that opportunity to balance and integrate the energy within you.

And that is how you release the Atlantean energies, heal your Atlantean Legacy and Paradigm, release your soul group, bring in new dimensional energies and integrate them.

So, what's next? How do we do this on a global and universal level and complete this journey? These are the next steps and we have already taken many of them.

Ascension -- Our Next Steps

Ascension is an energetic process in which we integrate new energetic frequencies to align with higher dimensions of being. We often talk about the density of the third dimension and that is because, relative to higher dimensions, the energy here is quite low, heavy and dense. Have you ever been around negative, fearful people and noticed that their energy makes you tired and irritable? That is an experience of dense energy and it can be very draining.

There are two ways of dealing with the dense energy; one is to avoid it, which is what we have done for many years. The other is more beneficial and more aligned with the ascension process, and that is to raise our energy so the density around us is either invited to participate at a higher level or it does not try to connect with us. Remember that ascension is a choice that everyone must make so we can offer others the choice of ascension, we just can't make them choose it. Those who are ready for ascension and who are open to this level of transformation will be grateful for this opportunity. Others will not be so accepting and may openly reject and judge you. Unable to connect to your higher energy, they are trying to bring your energy level down to theirs by making you angry, which makes it easier for them to connect with you at their level.

What are our next steps? Are we making progress and is the world, as it would appear, falling off the cliff as far as ascension goes? Not at all and we are making much progress at a very fast pace. The farther we go into the ascension cycle, the faster the energy moves and the more negative, fear-based energy is displaced. With fewer people willing to carry negative or lower vibrational frequencies, it can appear that there is a lot more negative energy than there actually is. What we are seeing is very concentrated negative energy within a few individuals or situations, and since we are not at those energetic levels any longer, any lower vibrating energies feel much more uncomfortable to us than they once did. The presence of lower vibrating energies is an invitation to keep our levels high and to remind ourselves that the light always wins over the darkness, it's just a matter of time and timing.

Earlier we read about the Atlantean Paradigm, the parameters that created the foundation of our ascension cycle, based on what we did in Atlantis. Let's take a look at those and see how we are progressing:

In the first parameter the dominant energy was masculine, which we have today. For centuries, women have been on the fringes of society, often denied participation and have suffered, as have their children, through the many wars, unrest, power plays and disruptions that have been created by the male energy as they fought each other for power and control. Their challenge was to integrate the feminine energy, which has not been done, until now. We are seeing more awareness among men of the need for balance between the two energies. Many men are accepting of this, some men are not. But the numbers are growing and especially with the new generations of Indigo and Crystal children, who are now young adults, we see a growing acceptance and integration of the feminine and a rejection of the exclusionary, war-like, dominant and controlling masculine energy.

And for their part, women are releasing their victim paradigm which is an aspect of their Atlantean Guilt and their Atlantis Legacy of remorse for the domination and control they once exerted over men. They are now accepting their power, insisting on equality in society and doing this in a spirit of cooperation and community with each other and with men.

This is one parameter that we are healing and in which we are moving beyond the Atlantean Paradigm's energies.

Are we more aware of our energy, gifts and talents? I believe we are, in ever greater numbers. With a shifting economic base and changing workplace dynamics, we no longer have the luxury of being unmotivated or waiting for someone to give us permission to do work that feeds our soul and allows us to use our gifts. As more workers lose their jobs, corporations downsize and the work scenario shifts, we need to be willing to acknowledge our gifts and talents so they can be shared with others because this is the new paradigm for the workplace today. The dramatic rise in people starting businesses, the creation of freelance work and the new, virtual nature of the workplace allows us to become self directed in our employment, which also mirrors what we did in Atlantis.

This is another paradigm that we are healing and in which we are incorporating some of the more positive aspects of Atlantis.

In the new ascension cycle, our ability to use our senses beyond the five physical senses was limited, as was our intuition and access beyond the veil directly into the spiritual world. We could no longer use these skills because of our previous carelessness and lack of respect for their power. Additionally, the ease with which we knew and used these gifts also made us complacent and take them for granted. We would be able to access them once we were at the level of understanding to be able to appreciate them. This has shifted dramatically in the past two decades and we now speak of 'spiritual' topics and understand ourselves as energetic beings. We have exceeded critical mass with respect to the level of humanity's willingness to accept spirit and to begin the process of integrating the ego and spirit.

This is another paradigm that we are healing and in which we are incorporating some of the more positive aspects of Atlantis.

Our ability to connect and communicate with our galactic community was taken away until we were more aware of our power and of the interconnection between us and the rest of the universe. We have had, over the last fifty years, many levels of communication with these beings although the vast majority have been denied or covered up by governments. In the coming months and years, more connection and communication will be possible and in a very short time, I believe we will have direct contact that cannot be covered up or denied.

We have healed this paradigm and are integrating the aspects and energies necessary to enable this as a potential for the near future.

The parameter which involved removing access to higher dimensions until we were ready was done for our benefit and safety, and not to punish us. Without being firmly grounded in the third dimension, we were unable to know the impact our actions would have in more dense and lower frequency energies. This is one reason why the ascension technology had such a disastrous effect, because the Earth's energy was still in 3D and the beam of light's effects would have been less damaging in a higher dimension environment. While it vastly limited our ability to heal and slowed the process of ascension considerably, keeping our awareness to a single dimension, until we were ready to have the awareness of higher dimensions, helped us manage our energy and our ascension path.

In the past several years we have been accessing higher dimensions on a limited basis. While these forays tend to have a strong physical impact, they also help us begin the alignment process and are proof of our progress.

We are quickly healing this paradigm and learning to integrate higher energetic frequencies to access higher dimensions of being with an understanding of our role within the greater scope of the universe and multidimensional realities.

The introduction of religion limited our direct access to Source until we were willing to reconnect and surrender the ego's fear. It was a strong lesson in humility, surrender, and power that has been the source of much of the world's pain and suffering in this ascension cycle. The ego and male dominated religious organizations have continued to use this power to put themselves in between humanity and its God/Source connection, rather than creating the belief systems that would promote our inner source connection and the concept of integrating divinity within our humanity. They have fulfilled their purpose, which was to compel us to choose our divinity in the form of a Source connection rather than thinking that the ego could become our God. It has been a long, painful, and sad journey but we have arrived. Religious institutions are quickly losing their power and we are shifting this paradigm through our increased spiritual awareness, acknowledgement of our inner divinity and intentional creation of a Source connection, as well as our desire to balance the ego's energy with spirit and create the human/divine partnership from which will emerge the ascended, spiritual human.

The dominance of the second dimension energy within the third, which created polarity, fear, and chaos has allowed us to recognize unconditional love, when we could choose it as an energetic alternative. This paradigm allowed us to experience the power of our free will and consciously choose to commit to ascension because we were living the alternative.

We are also healing and moving beyond this paradigm as we integrate unconditional love into our reality in the form of detachment, acceptance and non-judgment.

To create the paradigm which established a more confrontational, disconnected relationship between the Earth and humanity, the Earth had to embody and maintain third dimensional energies, relinquishing its access to higher dimensions, which created polarity in the Earth/human relationship. Now the Earth was a more hostile and less supportive environment, in which humanity had to struggle for survival. The lesson for humanity was to learn to love, honor and respect the Earth, a lesson which has taken a long time to learn. But we have learned it. We have come a long way on this journey and now see the Earth as it is, a sentient being who is our partner in ascension and as such, is an integral part of our ascension journey.

Our current focus on supporting the earth, preserving its resources, and safeguarding our planet is proof that we have shifted this parameter and are moving towards re-aligning with the Atlantean experience of living in harmony with the Earth as our partner in ascension and re-creating heaven on Earth.

The final parameter addressed how humanity would experience life. Instead of joy, abundance, freedom, and love, humanity would know pain and suffering on the course of their life path. This has been our experience of life for generations, until our recent acknowledgement of pain as one choice and unconditional love as a higher choice. As we integrate higher energetic frequencies into our realities, we will be less inclined to choose pain and suffering and more aware of the existence of higher aspects within each choice.

This has been one of our most challenging parameters because within the Atlantean Guilt paradigm is the belief that we do not deserve blessings, or joy or peace or love. We use this guilt to limit our access to more fulfilling, expansive ways of living because we believe that we should atone for our actions by suffering and victimizing ourselves. Through our Atlantis Legacy we have imagined our reality through the lens of our shame and remorse, limiting the use of our gifts because we don't want to misuse them. And the Atlantean Paradigm that we view as our punishment but was actually what we had to overcome, became the energetic prison that we thought limited our ability to access higher energetic frequencies and activate our direct Source connection. As we move out of judgment and into unconditional love, we will release the need to suffer and the belief that we should, and find more pleasant, fulfilling and joyful ways to experience life, which have always been available to us.

This parameter will be healed when we can see that suffering and pain are always a choice and we can also choose their higher aspects, joy and freedom at any time.

These new parameters set the foundation for the Earth's new ascension cycle, the one we are experiencing today. While it may appear that humanity was being punished for what it did in Atlantis, the opposite is true. All of the misuses of energy that were experienced created karma, or an energetic imprint, that had to be healed within the Earth's vibrational field. This healing is similar to the karmic healing that we do in lifetimes and karma can only be healed by its creator. So the collective karma that was created in Atlantis was part of the new ascension cycle and its healing had to be completed as part of the ascension journey.

And we are now at this time and place, on the threshold of yet another ascension cycle and at one of the most important moments in the history of ascension. What we do in this moment and in each moment will move us with greater momentum towards the completion of this ascension cycle. It is not a single choice that we make, but a choice that is made within every experience and on each step of that path. Seeking higher aspects within everything, acknowledging our power, affirming our divinity and maintaining our Source connection are all we need to do to enable ascension to move forward. Each one of us is the key to ascension, there is no one more powerful or capable, the final decision is not in the hands or heart of a single person. The human family, the Earth, the universes, our galactic community and all beings beyond are all watching us, supporting us with their intention for ascension as we move through these final stages and become our highest aspects, the spiritual human, an embodiment of the divine/human partnership. Then we create heaven on earth, move into higher dimensions of being and complete what we began in Atlantis, so long ago.

Final Thoughts For A New Beginning

Teaching about Atlantis has been an interesting journey for me, one I never thought I would embark on. And yet while I was preparing this information for the seminar I had agreed to teach, learning about Atlantis and all of the energy around it, I began to see so many parallels between what I was writing about and my own life. The many ways I limited my power, my soul group partners, including my family, the many ways I hesitated to use the accept the expression of my power, gifts and talents, suddenly all made sense. But the most profound discovery for me came, as I wrote in the book, when I understood the details of my Atlantis death and could relate it to my respect for water and fear of drowning, that I have had since childhood. That was the confirmation I needed to go more deeply into my Atlantis experience for answers to help me complete my ascension journey.

As we complete this cycle, and it is completing now, take heart in knowing that you are not alone, either in your fear, doubt and confusion, your experience of Atlantis, the healing work that needs to be completed now, your ascension path – all of these are aspects of everyone's life today, whether they are aware of them or not. We are on this journey together and have come too far to turn back. But we know so much and are so committed to this healing journey that this time we will succeed in opening the doorway to higher dimensions and creating heaven on earth.

I cannot stress enough how important your role is in ascension, even if you think you are just one small, insignificant person. You are so much more than that. Each of us is a spark of divine light, an expression of Creator in motion. You volunteered to be here at this time, from your love of Source and of humanity, your faith and trust, your desire to heal the Atlantis Paradigm and to experience ascension.

You are also ascending, it is part of you and what you do matters so much more than you can know. Don't lose faith or get discouraged, remember that everything has the potential to become its highest aspects when we know that those aspects exist and are willing to connect with them. We can become the masters that we are and have always been, by remembering ourselves as divine, deserving, and worthy of all that our heart desires . It is through our shared intention and collective desire for ascension that we will move beyond the third dimension, embrace our multi-dimensional potential, rejoin the galactic community and create heaven on earth.

Question and Answer

These questions were asked by students of the Healing the Paradigm seminar and they may answers some of the questions that you have about your own ascension journey.

Question: Are there spirits that are participating in this ascension?"

Answer: Absolutely. We have the entire body of the universe watching us and they can help us to a certain extent but they can't violate our free will, this was one of the parameters that was created for the beginning of this ascension cycle. As I'm saying free will I'm seeing a police scene that's marked with crime tape, sealing off a crime zone. They can stand at a respectful distance and help us but they cannot go beyond the crime tape. That's why what each of us does is important because we all have connections with different spiritual guides. We can pull in different energies. So the energetic connections that you open with your guides and your angels and other energetic beings that you communicate with share information with you but they cannot directly impact what happens here. When we open those connections, though, they work through and with each one of us.

Question: We got our light taken advantage of. Isn't that what's happening now with handing over our power to the government and corporations?"

Answer: Yes, it is exactly the same type of situation and it was set up as the Atlantean Paradigm, the parameters we had to work within to master this ascension cycle. We're aware of it and we are waking up. Look at the Occupy movement. What's it about? Taking back our power. The Arab Spring and its uprisings are about taking power back. The abuse of power has happened for a very long time. But what's the difference now? We know it. We're aware of it. Everyone is becoming aware of it. Being powerful, self-determination, a direct Source connection, integrating our divinity within our humanity is no longer an unfamiliar or forbidden concept. We're taking our power back. That's what the changes in the economy are doing. People that are losing their jobs and corporations aren't hiring anymore, banks aren't lending money anymore—that's all part of taking our power back. We can be controlled by banks or we can find a different way of operating. How can we do this in a different way that serves our needs, in spite of what they are doing? How can we come together and address our needs without relying on these corporate systems that have us convinced that we cannot operate without them?

Question: "The description of the Atlantis destruction mirrored a dream I had last year. Spooky!"

Answer: I have heard this from many people, including some whose dreams began to appear as soon as they signed up for the class. We are all on this journey together with a collective intention to heal the Atlantean Paradigm and to complete this ascension cycle in the best and highest way possible. To heal the paradigm we must know what we are healing, which is why so many memories of Atlantis are arising for you. It is a potential we can choose but with that knowledge, we can now choose something different.

Question: "Who is to say there will not be another attempt to harness everyone's power again?"

Answer: They will and they're trying to do that now. But so what? Let them try. It is the equivalent of having a child who is throwing a temper tantrum. What do you do? Well you can let the child cry and scream and yell or put the child in its room until they decide to act differently. Or you can say "Oh honey, what's wrong with you? What did Mommy do to make you so upset and how can I fix it? Here, have a cookie," which you know is going to empower them and now they know that they can throw a temper tantrum any time they want something. So they're going to try. So what? They can try but the only way we lose our power is when we give it away. No one can take our power from us. We give our power to them. We are sovereign in our lives and there is no way for anyone to take our sovereignty from us. They can't take your light from you. They can make you put your light out yourself or they can make you extinguish your own power or give your power away but they can't take it away from you.

If you are afraid of the darker energies you're just empowering them and through your fear you're going to give your power away. So don't give it away. Realize that you have the full force of the universe behind you. You have the entire galaxy and solar system and universe working with you. That's where your power lies.

Question: Will we get our Atlantean powers back, and when?

Answer: The short answer is "yes" but there are several stages to that answer. It depends on what we want and are willing to acknowledge. Who is going to say to you, "Here are your powers, you can take them now."? There is no one in the universe with that kind of authority over you. There is no graduation or ceremony to regain your power. I think we would like that but it isn't going to happen, at least not in a formal way. We get our powers back when we want them and know that we are ready for them.

The real question is "How much of your power are you comfortable with?" Much of this has to do with your soul group and when you are ready to forgive yourself and them, when you are comfortable with moving beyond them. You get your power back when you are comfortable with it, want it, and know that it won't or can't be taken away. You will be comfortable with this when you no longer fear that your power will be taken away or used against you, when you no longer want to share it with people who won't use it well or wisely. It's a matter of what you are comfortable with. How much power do you want? How much do you trust yourself to use it

143

wisely? And how confident are you that we are not going to repeat this lesson of Atlantis and we're not going to destroy ourselves and the world and everything in it?

Question: I was so emotional during the description of the destruction of Atlantis. Why is that?

Answer: For many of you, the moment in which you realized what was happening, how your power had been used, and how you participated in that destruction was very traumatic. But you shouldn't focus on it from the perspective of self blame. Some of you promised, in that dreadful moment, "I'll never do this again. I'll never use my power again. I won't use my gifts. I won't share my light. I'll never be taken advantage of again. No one is ever going to be able to use me in this way." And today, it's one of the ways that you prevent yourself from being used and taken advantage of. But you can pretend you don't have any power or you realize that you can be as powerful as you want to be. You just have to be very discerning about whom you share your power with.

Question: Has there been a stronger activation of our heart chakra recently?"

Answer: Yes. And you know I think we're trying to resolve the energies of our low heart chakra, which is the one we mostly operate out of and our high heart chakra, which is our spiritual heart chakra. Standing in between that though is this issue of deserving—"I deserve to be loved. I deserve to have this. I deserve to have my power back. I deserve to be able to love unconditionally and to receive that love in my life" but a lot of that is blocked by the Atlantean guilt and shame. So when we heal the Atlantean guilt and shame then we are able to open our heart chakra to receive higher energetic frequencies.

Question: Are we receiving messages or assistance or both, in the form of energetic downloads? Are these energies light or dark and should we be afraid of them?

Answer: That's a wonderful question and I first want to address the fear issue because we don't need to fear anything. Our fear opens us up energetically to a host of energies that we do not want to be associated with. As long as we stay out of fear, we keep our vibration high.

These energy downloads can be connected with in any way and can be integrated if we choose. What do you want, or are willing to have? Are you willing to allow yourself to have the full scope of that energy you had in Atlantis—to teleport, to telecommunicate, to be able to just whisk yourself off to wherever you want to go just by thinking of that place? Imagine sitting here and "I think I'll go have a coffee in Paris" and I'm sitting in a café and I'm right there. That's pretty awesome power. But because your power was so abused and the outcome was so destructive and you were part of it. Your families and friends were killed. You were killed. The world you loved was killed. You did a lot of damage to the Earth. You stopped ascension for the entire universe. It's pretty big responsibility. So look at all the guilt and shame that comes out of that.

But the enormity—the scope—of what we have done that we didn't intend to do… And it's one thing to intentionally create chaos and destruction and it's another to very innocently do something and the whole world falls apart because of it. Because the intention to create harm wasn't there it was very unconscious but it still happened and we were still a contributory element. That is what has prevented us from really accepting the full scope of the downloads, allowing ourselves to integrate a lot of energy versus what we think we can handle, what we think we can maintain control of, what we think we can be responsible for or use responsibly. We can easily integrate the higher energies that are available with these downloads when we are willing to allow ourselves to access that level of power, and set our intention to do so.

Question: What about the people who don't understand and accept this and who don't select this as part of their life path. what happens to them?

Answer: They have access to the same kind of information and energy that you do and they are getting it, in their own way. We cannot judge another's growth or life path because what we think is no growth at all may be an enormous leap in consciousness for them. We can't judge that in other people. We can't say, "Well because you're not here, listening to this information and have not said that you are ready to do this work, you are not ready for the ascension and are not participating." Someone's ascension journey may be that they acknowledge how they haven't used their power adequately or they're not very spiritually aware or acknowledging that they're not happy in their lives—that can be an enormous leap of consciousness for them. We will all ascend, in our own way and in our own time. This is part of our soul contract that is between us and our Source, and no one else.

This ascension process is available to everyone. There's no standard. So we have to be very careful about judging other people because we have no idea where they are on their soul path. That's between them and God. It's not between them and us. And the more that we are aware of them as part of the human family, the easier it's going to be for us to acknowledge this in ourselves and know that we are all ascending, but not in the same way. .

Question: Why was I so emotional as I heard about the destruction of Atlantis? I was sobbing and then felt this huge energy release.

Answer: It is a very emotional process for us because it was so traumatic. Many of us have buried or hidden these memories and they are quite painful when they arise. When we remember the transfer of power, that point where we shared our power, the betrayal, destruction, how much damage was done and how any people, including us, were killed, it is overwhelming.

The feeling of release came from letting go of these memories, of releasing yourself from the guilt and blame and finally letting go of the emotions that you have held on to for so many lifetimes.

Some of the comments mentioned how much of a difference this has made through the revelation of the Atlantean paradigm, understanding the soul group connections and realizing how you have been a martyred healer for them for so long and that you don't have to do that anymore so it can all be released to create a new paradigm for your life.

Question: Why did we give our power or share our power so willingly?

Answer: Because we thought it was going to benefit everyone by helping to conclude the ascension cycle. Remember that in Atlantis we had the memory of the previous ascension cycles and they also knew of this purpose and what they had to do to fulfill it. There was no separation between the spiritual and material worlds so there was no mystery in the process. And this knowledge made them lazy, so to speak, they didn't have to do any hard work, or so they thought. And they, I believe, just wanted to 'get it over with' and move on. They didn't value the process or realize its importance to the extent that we do now.

With so much power at their disposal, they did not value their power. So it was easy to share it with others. We do that when we give people our power and energy, we give them something they use for their own benefit and they do not value it. That's part of what healing this Atlantean Paradigm and legacy is about, realizing that if you give your power away, it goes to those who may not value it and who do not have the value systems in place to use the power in the best way. They will either squander it, misuse it or they'll use it against you. But they won't use it for their healing or yours.

Question: Is it OK to release my soul group now?

Answer: Yes you can and you are ready because you are asking the question. When you realize how you have embodied your Atlantean Paradigm with your soul group and limited your life in so many ways, it's time to transform that soul group experience by removing the energy that empowers it. When you do that the dynamics will change and you will be ready to accept that change in your life, no matter what it is. Releasing your soul group energy is about honoring yourself, honoring your journey and being clearer about your intention for your life.

What is your intention for your life and how do you honor yourself? Honoring yourself doesn't dishonor others. Honoring yourself simply honors you. And when you get out of that energy of atonement where you feel like you have to make up for what you've done or deny yourself out of feelings of guilt and shame then you really step into this new paradigm of living that actually allows ascension to occur because we can't raise the vibrations of the planet by lowering our own vibrations through guilt and shame.

Question: What happens if we fail at this ascension too, as we did in Atlantis?

Answer: We did not fail in Atlantis; we went as far as we could within the energetic frequencies that we held. There were different aspects of Atlantis that worked against ascension, even though they were put in place to assist in ascension. The only way that we can fail is to not integrate the energy necessary to reach higher dimensions, which is something we are all working on right now.

We can empower this process by stepping into our roles as the leaders and teachers and writers and healers and artists and creators that the world needs. We become a light for the world when we stand in our power. Then we become what we need to be, what the Earth and the universe needs, to allow this ascension to unfold in the way that it can and in the way that we have planned for this time.

I believe that this is one of the last attempts at ascension. We will be successful and I don't think it's going to be by a thread either. I think that what we are seeing in the world is the consolidation of energy and power but not so it can be misused or abused. That part of the paradigm is over, where we give our power to someone, a church, government or corporation, hoping they will take care of us. We did that and realized that when you give someone your power they won't take care of you. They'll take care of themselves with your power.

Question: How can we empower others without disempowering ourselves?

Answer: This is a great question and it's such a fine line that we walk when we try to help others. We empower others when we acknowledge their power and help them from that perspective, rather than feeling sorry for them and trying to fix them. That is the difference between compassion and pity. With compassion we shine our light so they can see it. With pity, we think they have no light and give them ours. Ascension requires that we acknowledge ourselves as powerful, divine beings and we empower others when we see that in them.

Question: How do I make a difference in the ascension cycle?

Answer: Each one of us is important. For example, when we did the exercise in which you were asked to expand yourself to become the full expression of our power, were you surprised at how big you got? If you feel small and insignificant it is because you are not fully expressing your power. when you do so and you see how much power you have, you will realize the difference you make and how important you are to the family of humanity. Your willingness to embody your power is exponentially magnified across the planet.

Since we are each an individualized expression of Source, when you are in the full expression of your power you allow Source to be in the full expression of its power through you. And then that expression is magnified across the planet and throughout the universe. Each of us is important and if we don't play our role then an important part of ascension is missing.

Question: I loved the expanding into your power exercise. I realized that this is why I couldn't set goals for myself or the future. I can finally honor myself because I know who I am.

Answer: One of the worst things we do to ourselves it to not acknowledge our power and divinity because that limits every aspect of our lives. And without seeing ourselves as powerful and with power, how can we set goals or achieve them? What is going to power our goals? If we can understand that our goals are another way that we allow Source to work through us, we stop seeing ourselves as small, insignificant and powerless. With Source as our source of power and our goals as the expression of this purpose through us, we can't fail.

Question: What is the difference between vibrations, beliefs and intention?

Answer: This is another good question. Vibrations are the energetic level you are at. In order to understand that better, let's create a scale from 1 to 10, where 1 is lowest and 10 is the highest vibration. Different energies represent different vibrations. For example, fear is a low vibrating energy, and for our purposes we will put it at a 1 on the scale. When you are in fear you are vibrating at a level of 1. Your vibration determines the other energies you attract, so you will be attracting things that match your one vibration.

Beliefs, which control your thoughts, set the level of your vibration. Every aspect of your belief system has a corresponding energetic vibration. If you believe you have to be afraid of your power or potential, your beliefs will set your vibration at the level of your fear and that is how you connect to the world. It's also how you attract corresponding energies. Whether you believe that you're capable of anything in the world or you're capable of nothing at all really depends on your beliefs, which set your vibration which then attracts things to you, or keeps them away from you.

Intention is how we use our thoughts, powered by our beliefs, to move energy. When you set an intention you set energy in motion to create it. Vibration, beliefs and intention all work together and they are how you create your reality.

About the Author

Jennifer Hoffman is a celebrated author, intuitive mystic, life and business mastery coach, international speaker, popular radio host and writes the celebrated Enlightening Life newsletter. Overcoming physical paralysis and survived a near fatal car accident taught Jennifer how to transcend fear and master limitations, hallmarks of her teachings, to achieve total confidence and personal fulfillment.

She is celebrated for her Enlightening Life newsletter, with more than two million weekly readers, and for her transformational work in helping others master their purpose to create joy, passion, success and abundance in life, love, career and business. Jennifer's books include the acclaimed Ascending into Miracles and 30 Days to Everyday Miracles.

A masterful teacher and transformational speaker, Jennifer leads seminars and workshops around the world. Learn more about Jennifer's work at www.enlighteninglife.com.

23936171R00093

Made in the USA
Middletown, DE
08 September 2015